TWAYNE'S WORLD AUTHORS SERIES

A Survey of the World's Literature

Sylvia E. Bowman, Indiana University
GENERAL EDITOR

CHINA

William R. Schultz, University of Arizona
EDITOR

Chou Tso-jen

(TWAS 184)

TWAYNE'S WORLD AUTHORS SERIES (TWAS)

The purpose of TWAS is to survey the major writers—novelists, dramatists, historians, poets, philosophers, and critics—of the nations of the world. Among the national literatures covered are those of Australia, Canada, China, Eastern Europe, France, Germany, Greece, India, Italy, Japan, Latin America, New Zealand, Poland, Russia, Scandinavia, Spain, and the African nations, as well as Hebrew, Yiddish, and Latin Classical literatures. This survey is complemented by Twayne's United States Authors Series and English Authors Series.

The intent of each volume in these series is to present a critical-analytical study of the works of the writer; to include biographical and historical material that may be necessary for understanding, appreciation, and critical appraisal of the writer; and to present all material in clear, concise English—but not to vitiate the scholarly content of the work by doing so.

Chou Tso-jen

By **ERNST WOLFF**
University of Illinois

Twayne Publishers, Inc. :: New York

To the
sustaining love and patience
of
Kuei-ch'ing,
Martin and Peter

Preface

Chou Tso-jen left his mark on Chinese literary history, particularly as one of the most accomplished and most impressive proponents of the new art of modern essay writing. However, beyond that, Chou was a relevant force in modernizing the whole of Chinese literature, introducing new concepts of art, of the function of literature, and even of the nature of society and man in society in general.

As we examine some of these "new" concepts today, they may appear already out of date, the expressions of an effete liberalism of a past era, but his liberalism and inherent humanitarianism helped bring enlightenment where a narrow traditionalism blocked the path of progress.

Among contemporary Chinese intellectuals there were few indeed who did not come under the influence of his writings, but there were also few who would later acknowledge their indebtedness. For political reasons Chou became "inopportune" on Taiwan, as well as on the mainland, and as a consequence his name has been suppressed in all of China.

Abroad, the name of the man who had been one of the greats of the literary stage of his time is now hardly known. All these circumstances would appear amply to justify an attempt at analysis and evaluation of the work and the significance of this man.

To attempt this task is certainly a presumptuous undertaking for a non-Chinese. The lack of a Chinese cultural background and linguistic inadequacies are formidable obstacles, particularly in approaching the works of Chou Tso-jen, whose personality is so deeply rooted in Chinese tradition and whose art depends to such a great extent upon stylistic finesse and nuances of expression, so easily lost on the foreigner. Nevertheless, it is hoped that a genuine admiration for a great artist and humanitarian, and perhaps an "outsider's" less biased viewpoint, may compensate for these deficiencies.

The subjectivity of all literary evaluation was one of Chou Tso-jen's tenets, and it is one to which this study will also gladly subscribe. The conclusions reached need therefore not be concurred in by everyone, but the study will still not have been in vain if it will at least have demonstrated in a humble way the deserved place that Chou should occupy in China's literary and cultural history.

78412

Contents

Chronology

1885 Born on January 16, Shaohsing, Chekiang Province.
1893 Grandfather Chou Fu-ch'ing imprisoned, family impoverished.
1897 Father dies; Chou Tso-jen moves to Hangchow.
1901 Enters Nanking Naval Academy.
1905 Visits Peking for government examination; qualifies for studies abroad.
1906 To Japan as student on government stipend.
1909 Marries Habuto Nobuko, a Japanese, in Tokyo.
1911 Returns to China.
1912 Teacher of English at Shaohsing.
1917 Moves to Peking; professor of literature at National Peking University.
1918 Contributes essays to various literary magazines, particularly the *Hsin-ch'ing-nien*.
1919 Revisits Japan; meets Mushakoji Saneatsu.
1921 Cosponsor of the Literary Research Society and regular contributor to the magazine *Hsiao-shuo yüeh-pao*.
1923 *Tzu-chi ti yüan-ti* (One's Own Garden), an anthology of essays, published.
1924 Co-organizer of the *Yü-ssu* literary society.
1925 *Yü-t'ien ti shu* (A Rainy Day's Book).
1927 *T'an lung chi* (Speaking of Dragons).
1928 *T'an hu chi* (Speaking of Tigers).
1931 Becomes Dean of the Department of Japanese Literature at National Peking University.
1932 Contributes essays to *Yü-chou-feng, Jen-chien-shih, Lun-yü* magazines.
1934 Visits Japan. *Yeh-tu-ch'ao* (Notes from Night Reading).
1937 Lukouch'iao incident; decides to stay on in Peking.
1939 Escapes assassination attempt with only minor injuries.

Chronology

1940 Appointed Commissioner of Education in the Japanese-sponsored North China regime.

1944 *K'u-k'ou kan-k'ou* (Bitter and Sweet).

1945 Brought to Nanking; tried and convicted for collaboration with the enemy.

1949 Released from prison at Shanghai; eventually returns to Peking to his former home.

1955 *Lu Hsün ti ku-chia* (Lu Hsün's Old Home), reminiscences of common childhood at Shaohsing.

1962 Wife dies in Peking.

1966 Dies in November, according to a report published in a Hong Kong magazine.

CHAPTER 1

Biography

CHOU Tso-jen was born on January 16, 1885, in the city of Shaohsing, Chekiang Province.[1] He was originally given the name K'uei-shou. His *tzu,* or courtesy name, was Ch'i-ming. The pseudonyms he used at various times in his long career number over thirty; those most frequently employed were Chih-t'ang and Ch'i-ming (in characters different from his courtesy name). His so-called studio names were K'u-ch'a-an (Bitter-Tea Hermitage) and K'u-yü-chai (Bitter-Rain Studio). After 1949, Chou consistently used the pen name Chou Hsia-shou.

His family was of higher middle-class standing; the clan traced its ancestry back to the early sixteenth century and had produced a number of scholar-officials over the years. The clan records indicate that his branch of the family moved to the Shaohsing area during the Ming dynasty. Chou Tso-jen belonged to the fourteenth generation, counting from the first historical ancestor.[2]

At about six years of age, Chou began to receive instruction from the family teacher at his native place. When he was about eleven, he was enrolled in a larger private school, where for the next three years he was occupied in the traditional study of the Chinese classics.[3] Two years earlier, his grandfather, an official and the family's main provider, was arrested and imprisoned for attempted bribery; he had tried to buy the favor of one of his son's examiners.[4] As a result, the family fell on hard times; the family finances were further aggravated by the long illness of his father, who died in 1897. Chou was then sent to live with relatives in Hangchow.

In August, 1901, Chou Tso-jen followed his elder brother Chou Shu-jen—who was later to become a famous writer and critic

1

under the pen name Lu Hsün—to Nanking. There he entered the
Naval Academy, where he was assigned to a program to study in
marine engineering.[5] Upon the completion of his studies at the
Naval Academy, he was sent with twenty-three of his classmates
to Peking to sit for a government scholarship examination.[6] He
passed successfully and was sent to Japan for further studies in
1906.[7] He traveled with his elder brother Lu Hsün, who had been
in Japan since 1902 and had recently returned to Shaohsing to be
married.

Upon the completion of a program of preparatory courses at
Hosei University, Chou Tso-jen was advised to transfer to the
civil engineering department because of poor vision. Since he felt
more and more drawn to the study of literature, when he later
began formal academic studies at Rikkyō University, he under-
took the study of European literature; in order to acquire a broad
understanding of European literature and culture, he also began
at that time the study of classical Greek. At the same time, he
took a strong interest in the contemporary literature of his host
country, Japan. In all his studies and reading at that time, he
acquired an ever growing interest in and appreciation of the new
ideas and new literary forms then being introduced into Japan
from the West.

This was also a time when groups of Chinese political refugees
were active in Japan, publishing revolutionary articles and books,
and lecturing to young Chinese students, to arouse in them a sense
of national consciousness and to prepare them for active participation in the political affairs of the home country. As far as Chou
was concerned, these influences motivated him to explore in particular the literary expressions of underprivileged and politically
enslaved countries, because of similarities he saw between their
situation and that in which China then found itself.

In 1909, Chou married a Japanese, Habuto Nobuko, in
Tokyo.[8] It is said that this additional burden on the family
finances forced his brother Lu Hsün, then the eldest male in the
family and therefore responsible for its well-being, to return to
China in 1909 to help provide for its welfare.[9] In his autobiography, Lu Hsün mentions in particular that he was forced to
give up his plans to go to Germany for further studies.[10] As late
as 1968, a former Chou family servant reminiscing of that time

claims to remember that Lu Hsün used to remit sixty Chinese dollars per month to his brother in Japan.[11]

In 1911, Chou Tso-jen himself returned to China without having formally completed his studies.[12] He was first appointed a school inspector and later a teacher of English at a middle school in his native Shaohsing. In April, 1917, he went to Peking at the urging of his brother Lu Hsün, who had previously arrived in Peking as a member of the staff of the Ministry of Education.[13] Ts'ai Yüan-p'ei had recently assumed the presidency of Peking National University and was then in the process of making it into a modern educational institution.[14] He was eager to add promising young men to the faculty, and he appointed Chou as an instructor of Greek, Roman, and modern European literature.[15] Later, Chou also lectured at other institutions in Peking, but he remained on the faculty of Peking University until 1937, with a brief interruption only in 1927 during the period of the Chang Tso-lin regime, when the political situation forced him to remain inactive for about one year.[16]

On joining the faculty of Peking National University in 1917, Chou immediately entered an intellectually stimulating environment. Under the liberal and progressive leadership of Ts'ai Yüan-p'ei, its president, Peking National University attracted to its campus actively progressive intellectuals like Ch'en Tu-hsiu,[17] Hu Shih,[18] Ch'ien Hsüan-t'ung,[19] Liu Pan-nung,[20] and others. Despite frequent social and political repression, the decade between 1917 and 1927 was a vital, stimulating era and proved on the whole to be a very fruitful and happy time in his life.[21] In the congenial atmosphere of Peking University and among men devoted, like himself, to modern ideas and cultural and social change, he reached full maturity of character and mind and perfected his skill as an essayist.

During this initial period of his literary life, Chou contributed translations, and later essays, to literary journals of national standing and periodicals of social comment, such as *Hsin-ch'ing-nien* (New Youth), *Hsin-ch'ao* (New Tide), *Mei-chou p'ing-lun* (Weekly Critic), *Shao-nien Chung-kuo* (Young China), and the literary supplement of the *Peking Morning Post*.[22] He was also instrumental in organizing a periodical devoted to the collection of folk songs, the *Ko-yao chou-k'an* (Folk Song Weekly),[23] an indication of his early interest in this branch of popular art.

In 1919, Chou had his first opportunity to revisit Japan. On this occasion, he met Mushakoji Saneatsu, a meeting that resulted in a lifelong friendship between the two men. Mushakoji was the leading writer of the so-called Shirakaba group, which took its name from the periodical *Shirakaba* (White Birch). The magazine flourished from 1910 to 1923; in it were published numerous articles espousing the ideals of individualism, liberalism, and humanitarianism.[24] It was during this trip to Japan that Chou also visited the *Atarashiki mura* (New Village), a community project of the Mushakoji group organized along humanitarian, Socialist lines, which impressed him very much as a courageous attempt to realize ideals to which he too subscribed.[25]

In 1921, Chou spent half a year recuperating from an illness at the Pi-yün-ssu, a temple located in a scenic setting near Peking. The same year saw the formal inauguration of the Literary Research Society,[26] in which he was one of the leading spirits and for which he composed the inaugural manifesto on an "Art for Life's Sake" theme.[27] He also became a regular contributor of the *Hsiao-shuo yüeh-pao* (Short Story Monthly) and wrote for it as long as it remained the organ of the Literary Research Society.[28]

In 1923, a family quarrel, apparently arising from a disagreement between the two wives, resulted in Lu Hsün moving away from the house the two families had jointly occupied until that time. Hsü Kuang-p'ing, Lu Hsün's wife, later recorded her version of the quarrel in *Lu Hsün hui-i-lu* (Recording Memories of Lu Hsün).[29] Ever after she retained a lifelong hatred for Chou Tso-jen. It is noteworthy that she later achieved a certain eminence in Communist China as the widow of Lu Hsün, the literary idol of that government. An anti-Chou Tso-jen article written by her in the course of the so-called Cultural Revolution, and only a few months before her own death in 1968, was given great prominence in the *People's Daily* of October 19, 1967. The heading of her vituperation of Chou was: "Our Ulcer [meaning Chou Tso-jen] is their [meaning the "reactionaries"] Treasure." However, between the two brothers themselves there does not seem to have been a lasting rift as a consequence of this quarrel. In 1924, they again cooperated in organizing the *Yü-ssu* Society, with such other members as Lin Yutang,[30] Ch'ien Hsüan-t'ung, Liu Pan-nung, and Sun Fu-yüan.[31] Chou Tso-jen became editor-in-chief and one of the main contributors to the *Yü-ssu* (Threads of Talk) weekly magazine, which survived until March, 1930, when the police banned it for political reasons.[32] Its successor, the *Lo-t'o-ts'ao* (Camel Grass), was more in the nature of a personal venture of Chou Tso-jen, who, during its short life from May to October, 1930, served as its editor-in-chief.

For his well-known liberal to leftist ideas, Chou was suspect to the warlord governments of North China. In 1926, the Tuan Ch'i-jui government blacklisted him, together with about fifty other professors.[33] In 1927, when Chang Tso-lin assumed control of the Peking government, Chou felt himself in even more serious danger and took refuge—together with Liu Pan-nung—in the house of the Japanese military attaché in Peking.[34] In 1929, he suffered a grave family misfortune; his youngest daughter, of whom he had been extremely fond, died of illness at the age of fifteen.[35] He was left with one son and one daughter.[36]

As early as 1927, internal political and social developments began to dampen Chou's usually optimistic outlook on life, and signs of personal disillusionment and despair became noticeable. Even the hoped-for "progressive forces" moving up from the South had shown even before reaching Peking ominous tendencies to use terror as an instrument of government.[37] Most depressing to him was the constant harassment of and hostility toward intellectuals shown by the warlord rulers of North China and their suppression of the freedom of literary expression. Under these circumstances, Chou declared that he would simply close his door to the events of the day and retire to a life of quiet scholarship. The studies undertaken during this self-imposed semiretirement from the literary scene no doubt deepened his knowledge and understanding of the literary and philosophical heritage of China, and also, to a lesser degree, of Japan, whose literature continued to command his active attention.

In 1931, Chou was appointed dean of the new Department of Japanese Literature at Peking University. It must have been a gratifying appointment, because cultural rapprochement between the two peoples had always been one of his goals. Unfortunately, the political situation made it a rather inappropriate time for efforts to introduce Japanese cultural values to the Chinese. In 1934, he had another opportunity to visit Japan. For a period of two months he studied at first hand Japanese literature and education. By then he must have been fairly well known in Japan, as testified to by the large circle of friends that welcomed him upon his arrival.[38]

During the period 1932–37, Chou regularly contributed articles to the *Yü-chou-feng* (The Cosmic Wind) and occasionally to *Jen-chien-shih* (This Human World) and *Lun-yü* (Analects), all magazines edited by his good friend Lin Yutang. For the period 1936–37, a number of his essays are also to be found in a short-lived periodical called *I-ching* (Unorthodox Classics), which was published in Shanghai.

The Lukoch'iao incident of 1937 also brought great changes in his life. When the Japanese occupied North China, they closed down Peking National University because of known anti-Japanese feelings among intellectuals and students. A large percentage of its student body and an estimated 1,500 faculty members of various northern universities migrated to unoccupied areas.[39] Chou Tso-jen, however, decided to stay in Peking.

Hu Shih, who was then dean of Peking National University's Faculty of Arts and attending a meeting in South China, first advised his colleagues in the north to devote themselves to scholarly work during this time of enforced leisure.[40] Later, however, Hu Shih addressed a letter to Chou Tso-jen, in which he urged Chou to move out of North China.[41] In order to avoid Japanese censorship, the letter was couched in a cryptic poetical style which would translate somewhat as follows:

> In last night's dream I clearly saw
> A Buddhist priest with cup in hand
> Stand in your studio sipping tea.
> Then suddenly the cup was left and out he went
> As wafted by a breeze of wind, with cane in hand,
> South, further south, mile upon mile,
> How much discomfort in a trip like this!
> If wise enough, a man can judge what matters most.
> The dream has passed, I cloak myself and gaze outside.
> This longing for my friend, who but myself can feel!

Chou replied in much the same style, declining to follow Hu Shih's advice:

The Old Monk may pretend to relish "bitter tea"
But actually 'tis naught but "bitter rain"!
Recently the roof began to leak, the floor to flood,
And in the end we can't but call it "bitter stay"!

When spreading out my mat tonight to go to sleep
An unexpected letter came from far away:
Eight lines of poetry from distances that spread like sea and sky.
I thank the recluse Tsang Hui for his inquiry
And gratefully acknowledge his affection!
Too sad, the pilgrimage cannot be done;
Not that his duties keep the monk too occupied,
But in this monastery live the aged and the very young.
All I can do is: close my door, beat the *mu-yü,* and chant my prayers,
And make my rounds with beggar's bowl in hand,
Collecting rice and flour for my sustenance.
Old Monk will always be Old Monk,
My only hope: I may be able still
To look into your eyes some day again! [42]

"Bitter tea" and "bitter rain" are allusions to two of Chou's studio names. The name Tsang Hui in the eighth line is one of Hu Shih's pseudonyms. The *mu-yü* mentioned in the thirteenth line is a drum used by Buddhist priests to beat time when chanting prayers. The Chinese version of the last line has a strong connotation of "being able to look you straight in the eye" without any feeling of guilt or shame, an assurance that nothing shameful will occur.

The reasons for his decision to remain in Peking were stated in a letter to the editor of *Yü-chou-feng,* which was published in its July 1, 1938, issue. There he states that he found himself burdened with responsibility for nine members of his own and his brothers' families, some too old and some too young to risk the difficult journey into unoccupied territory. Only much later in a letter dated February 10, 1966, and sent from Peking to his friend Hsü Hsü in Hongkong, did he explain the situation in more detail. His household at that time in Peking consisted of: "Myself, my wife, my son, and my daughter. My daughter was married, but her husband was in Sian, so she stayed in my house together with her two sons. My younger brother's 'abandoned' wife, who was my wife's younger sister, with two sons and one daughter, also lived at our place. Then, there was also my mother and Lu Hsün's widow, who, though living apart, expected me to look after them. Even without counting them, but including myself, there were already ten people. . . . Therefore, it was best to remain in Peking and 'live in bitterness.' " [43]

The decision to remain in Peking may also have been influenced by personal experience. He had had long and sometimes happy associations with the Japanese people, and he greatly admired certain aspects of Japanese culture. His attitude toward the Japanese did not assume the same degree of hatred or horror shown by many of his countrymen at the mere thought of having to live under a Japanese-dominated regime. His knowledge of the Japanese language and customs also gained new importance, for this enabled him to intervene effectively on behalf of Chinese interests with the Japanese military administration. It must have been obvious to him that there was a need for men of his qualifications to remain in the occupied areas and try, to the best of their abilities, to mitigate the harshness of Japanese military rule and thus maintain and defend Chinese rights and property, as was possible only with a knowledge of Japanese and with an understanding of the Japanese mentality. One incident of his personal intervention with the Japanese authorities was reported at the time by a refugee from North China in an issue of the *Yü-chou-feng* magazine (No. 74 of Sept. 1, 1938).

On New Year's Day, 1939, an attempt was nevertheless made to assassinate Chou. His ricksha-puller was killed, but Chou himself luckily escaped serious injury. The assailant was never caught. The Japanese blamed the incident on the Chinese Communists or nationalists.[44] Some Chinese have accepted this interpretation of the incident. Liu Hsin-huang, for instance, concludes that the incident made Chou more receptive to Japanese overtures for cooperation,[45] an opinion that is also shared by Hung Yen-ch'iu.[46] Chou Tso-jen himself, however, accused the Japanese military of the crime, because their tight control of the city at the time made a crime of this nature almost impossible to carry off and made the escape of the criminals highly unlikely without official connivance.[47] Their motive, according to Chou, was the fear that his antagonism to Japanese military operations could have great influence upon Chinese intellectuals remaining in the city, even on liberally minded Japanese. During his trial in 1947, Chou adduced this incident to prove that his hostile attitude toward the Japanese military was known to them. He also contended that he was coerced into serving the Japanese-sponsored puppet regime of North China, the threat to his life having been very real.

Peking National University was reopened January 14, 1939, with only four science departments, but, when in August of the same year a department of literature was added, Chou was appointed as its head.[48] On the death of T'ang Erh-ho, the incumbent minister of education of the Japanese-sponsored North China regime, Chou Tso-jen was appointed to that position. The appointment is recorded in No. 47/48 (February 4, 1941) of the *Gazette of the North China Government,* as being effective from January 4, 1941. About two years later, in its issue of April 19, 1943 (No. 201/202), the *Gazette* reports the assumption of the office of minister of education by Su T'i-jen, Chou's successor, as beginning on February 10, 1943. Therefore, Chou's term of office came to an end at that time. It is difficult now to ascertain—and this is not the time or place to pass judgment—whether and to what extent personal pressures were brought to bear on him in this instance, or whether his collaboration with the Japanese military was altogether reasoned and voluntary. There is no doubt, however, that his name added prestige to the puppet regime and that, once involved in public functions, additional commitments were hard to avoid. In April, 1941, Chou visited Japan as a delegate to the East Asia Cultural Conference.[49] The *Hsin Chung-kuo shou-ts'e* (New China Handbook) of November, 1942 lists Chou Tso-jen as a Central Committee member of the Japanese-sponsored New People's Party and as honorary chairman of the Chinese Education Reconstruction Association, a Japanese front organization. The *Shen-pao Yearbook* of 1944 (p. 988) also mentions him as being a member of the New Literature Study Association, an organization also sponsored by the Japanese. He is also listed as president of an East Asia Cultural Association in *Chūgoku shinshi roku* (Directory of Eminent Chinese), which was compiled by Nakanishi Rihachi and published in 1942 by the Man-Mō Shizai Kyōkai (Association for Manchurian-Mongolian Resources).

Following the Allied victory over Japan, Chou was brought to Nanking and tried for collaboration with the enemy.[50] During the trial, his strongest support came from Hu Shih. "Hu not only denied that Chou had been a traitor, but he even made him out to be a 'loyal minister.' Hu Shih actively collected evidence to support his contention that Chou, by remaining in Peking, had effectively protected the property of Peking National University." [51] The fact that Peking National University had indeed benefited materially during the period of occupation was attested to in an article published in the *Shanghai Evening Post and Mercury* on

December 20, 1946, which reads in part: "Peita (Peking National University) is the most fortunate of the returned government universities in Peiping, or for that matter, in the whole of North China. Its physical plant is not only intact but has increased in size, as the puppet authorities added to its buildings as well as its library."

During the trial, Chou appears to have maintained an undaunted spirit. In an essay entitled "Lao-hu-ch'iao pien k'an Chih-t'ang" (Meeting Chou Tso-jen in Nanking Prison), which was published in *Chin-fan chi-wai,* Huang Shang quotes a quatrain composed by Chou at that time which reads as follows:

> The painting of the plum flower is for all to view,
> But the spirit that guided the brush is difficult to fathom,
> Just as in the case of "Poetry at the Black Tower,"
> When Su Shih's bearing and mien were not of the ordinary.

The "Poetry at the Black Tower" refers to an episode in the life of the famous Sung dynasty poet Su Shih (A.D. 1037–1101), who preserved his peace of mind and aloofness toward his accusers when unjustly incarcerated.[52]

According to a report in the Shanghai *Ta-kung-pao* (L'Impartial) of November 17, 1946, Chou Tso-jen was sentenced to fourteen years' imprisonment; the report furthermore states that the Court considered a life sentence justified, but exercised leniency in view of certain acts by which Chou had "benefited the people during the period of enemy occupation." On November 30, the same newspaper reported that Chou had appealed the sentence. There is no account of the result of that appeal, although the sentence finally imposed seems to have been ten years in prison.[53] However, owing to the changing political situation, he did not have to serve even the reduced term. Transferred to Shanghai together with other collaborators, he was subsequently released in the course of a general amnesty, by which the Shanghai authorities tried to relieve congestion in the city prisons. Perhaps his release was merely a last gesture of magnanimity on the part of the Kuomintang authorities, because by all appearances power was in any case soon to pass into the hands of the advancing Communist armies. It has also been suggested that his early release from prison was due to the personal intervention of Li Tsung-jen, who had shortly before replaced Chiang Kai-shek as president and was desperately trying to broaden his political following.[54]

•

After his release from prison, Chou spent most of 1949 in Shanghai. He made inquiries about a possible move to Taiwan, but for some reason arrangements could not be completed before the occupation of the city by the Communists.[55] Soon afterward he returned to Peking and his wife and family at his former home at No. 8, Pa-tao-wan. The new situation in which he then found himself must have been an extremely delicate one. To support his family, he had no recourse but to try to reestablish himself as a writer. On the other hand, there was no longer a place for his kind of literary art, nor was he a man to submit lightly to discipline and directives where art was concerned. Moreover, he enjoyed the uncertain distinction of having been stigmatized by Mao Tse-tung himself, who, in his "Lectures at the Yenan Symposium on Literature and Art" (1942), had labeled Chou as a writer of "slave literature." That he was allowed to exist at all was perhaps due to the fact that he was the brother of Lu Hsün, who had been elevated posthumously to the position of literary idol of the new regime, or ties of friendship, or to the traditional Chinese respect for the *lao-shih* (old teacher), since many members of the government had been his students at Peking National University. Hsü Kuang-p'ing, in the diatribe mentioned earlier, alleged that high party officials in Peking, among them Chou Yang and Hu Ch'iao-mu, had protected and supported him and that his personal diary had been purchased for preservation in the Peking Lu Hsün Museum.

Even though he must have benefited from certain influences in his favor, his existence was at best precarious. Most of his former colleagues ignored him. The well-known writer Ah-ying, for instance, had all references to him expunged from the 1955 edition of his *Wan Ch'ing hsiao-shuo shih* (History of Late Ch'ing Fiction), as a comparison with the prewar edition of the same book will reveal. In 1956, Liu Shou-Sung published *Chung-kuo hsin-wen-hsüeh ch'u-kao* (Tentative Outline of Modern Chinese Literature) with chapters on the Literary Research Society and the Chinese Essay without once mentioning the name of Chou Tso-jen. J. Prusek in his "Basic Problems of the History of Modern Chinese Literature" shows a strong anti-Chou bias for other than literary reasons.[56] It is understandable, therefore, that in this hostile atmosphere Chou had to be wary in choosing topics for his essays and books. Not unwisely, he limited himself to translations and studies of Greek and Japanese literature and folklore and to writing on the Chou family history as it pertained to his deceased older brother, Lu Hsün. It is all the more remarkable that he was still able to publish as much as he did. Hsu Kuang-p'ing, who can be trusted to be accurate in this respect, has enumerated eleven individual items from his pen, all written and published since 1949 by the Peking People's Literature Publishing Company; another six items of translation were said to have been ready for printing but were apparently held up by the so-called Great Proletarian Cultural Revolution.

In the 1950's and early 1960's, Chou maintained a lively correspondence with many friends living abroad, particularly in Hong Kong and Japan. Some of his letters written during these years have since been published in such Hong Kong magazines as *Pi-tuan* (Quill), *Ming-pao* (Ming-pao Monthly), and *Ch'un-ch'iu tsa-chih* (The Observation Post); but judging from other specimens examined by the author, much of this correspondence still awaits publication. When these letters become available for study, additional light will be shed on his last years in Peking. A few of his friends from Hong Kong and Japan who were able to visit him in Peking reported that he lived under much reduced circumstances.[57]

In the spring of 1967, Chinese periodicals in Hong Kong reported his death, which is purported to have occurred during November, 1966.[58]

CHAPTER 2

The Chinese Essay

THE essay, the literary medium in which Chou Tso-jen achieved his fame, is usually defined as an informal account of personal experience or opinion in a comparatively short piece of prose writing.[1] By its very nature, one might be led to assume that man's first literary impulses resulted in the essay. On the contrary, however, the essay appeared rather late as a distinct literary genre. In Europe, for instance, its inception is usually dated from the late sixteenth century and connected with the name of Michel de Montaigne.[2] The reason for the late appearance of the essay on the literary scene may have been a general attitude of disdain for informal expression, an attitude that was even more pronounced in China than in the West.

Early Chinese prose is mainly either historical narrative or philosophical discourse, but even where, beyond the informative and didactic, true esthetic value is discernible, as in the parables of Chuang-tzu,[3] or in the later anecdotes of the *Shih-shuo hsin yü* (Sayings of the World),[4] these writings cannot be regarded as essays in the formal sense, because they show little personal involvement on the part of the author. In fact, personal ostentation in language other than poetry seems to have been frowned upon by the didacticism characteristic of Chinese antiquity. Only after the fall of the Han dynasty, when substantial changes occurred in the social climate, did a new trend toward individualism and estheticism become noticeable in literature, as evidenced, for instance, in the unconventional spirit of the Seven Masters of the Chien-an period (196–219)[5] or in the literary theories of Ts'ao P'i (187–226).[6] The same age also witnessed the budding of the lyrical essay.[7] The period of the Six Dynasties which followed the Han

13

period produced an abundance of essays in many varying forms.[8]

There were the *shu* (letters), in which communications were exchanged in a rather ornate and elaborate style. Most examples of the form are discursive and spirited in manner. The *hsü* (preface) and *po* (postscripts) to his own or another writer's work frequently assumed the form of a short essay in itself, in which the writer at times digressed into personal reflections on life and fate. To mention only two examples, there are the famous "Orchid Pavilion Preface" by Wang Hsi-chih (321–79)[9] and T'ao Yüanming's (365–427) equally famous "Peach Spring Preface." [10] We also see during this period the traditional *chi* (record) of impersonal historiography branch out into separate forms: the very personal *pi-chi* (literary notebook) [11] and *jih-lu* (diary), which are both in essence true essay forms.

The *chuan* (biography), which is basically not an essay, is a record of an individual's life. However, there are instances when such recordings assume essay form, as, for instance, in the case of T'ao Yüang-ming's autobiographical and lyrical *Wu Liu hsiensheng chuan* (Biography of Mr. Five-Willows).

The *shuo* (discourse) [12] seems to have evolved from philosophical disputation; later it also came to be used as a medium for political persuasion. Although often employed for utilitarian purposes, examples of the form frequently contain embellishments and digressions, and thereby it assumes the appearance of an essay on a political topic. As we find all these various types of prose writing well represented in the *Wen-hsüan* anthology,[13] we may truly regard the Six Dynasties period as the beginning of the Chinese essay.

During the succeeding dynasties, various writers made their respective contributions to the further development of the essay. Two of the most eminent prose writers of the T'ang dynasty, Han Yü (768–824) and Liu Tsung-yüan (773–819),[14] both of whom were proponents of greater naturalness and individualistic expression in literature, produced many prose pieces that qualify as essays, both in form and in substance. Famous men of letters of the Sung dynasty,[15] such as Ou-yang Hsiu, Su Tung-p'o, and Wang An-shih, all utilized effectively various essay forms, as for instance letters, postscripts, funerary tablets, travel records, diaries, and so on. A specialized form, the essay of literary criticism (*shih-hua*), also flourished in the Sung dynasty, a time when, "nourished by the abundance of exquisite poetry if the T'ang and deepened by Zen Buddhism, Chinese literary criticism reached a climax." [16]

During the several centuries of Ming rule, the essay declined as a form under the domination of the *pa-ku wen* (eight-legged essay) style,[17] a form characterized by uniform structural rules. Toward the close of the dynasty, the resurgence of naturalness and simplicity of manner resulted from new concepts of literary value propounded by the Kung-an and Ching-ling literary schools.[18] In their repudiation of orthodox standards of literary value and espousal of progressive and individualistic ideals, these writers anticipated in various ways reformist-minded cultural leaders of the present century. As a result, some literary historians, including Chou Tso-jen,[19] place the inception of the modern Chinese essay with these two literary schools.

It is to be doubted, however, that the average modern reader finds the language and style of these late Ming dynasty writers sufficiently close and intimate, or their topics of sufficiently acute present-day interest, to designate them as "moderns." Instead, it may be more justified to designate as modern essays those compositions that are written in the contemporary language, the *pai-hua*.[20] It is in this sense that we conclude that China's *modern* essay was one of the achievements of the so-called Chinese Renaissance, the cultural facet of the May Fourth Movement, in which Chou Tso-jen too was an active participant.

CHAPTER 3

Early Motivation Toward Literature and the Essay

C HOU'S first contact with the literature of his country was naturally an early one, a consequence of his being brought up in a scholar-gentry family of traditional type. As was customarily the case, his first school books were the *Ssu-shu* (the "Four Books") and the *Wu-ching* (the "Five Classics"),[1] but the classics were certainly not his exclusive reading material. The family libraries, even of the strictly Confucian gentry, usually contained much that could also satisfy youthful longings for adventure or inspire by pure beauty or stimulate imagination and fantasy.

One of Chou's early memories, for instance, is of a picture book, the *Ch'i-ch'iao-t'u,*[2] on which he remarks as follows:

the most unforgettable of all books that I amused myself with when I was very small. I recollect that I had only a very common . . . bookshop copy of it, but several of its pictures, as, for instance, the "Lotus Leaves and Fish," in their simple purity and sincerity had something classical about them. It is for this reason that I cannot forget them.[3]

Later, Chou came to discover the novel, which in China as all over the world is apt to provide adventure, romance, and knowledge of the world beyond home and native place for the healthy curiosity of the adolescent. Chou's account runs as follows:

I started very late to read novels, when I was about eleven or twelve years old. The one I read first, I remember, was the *Ching-hua-yüan* (Flowers in the Mirror),[4] thereafter, it was probably *Hsi-yu-chi* (Journey to the West), *Feng-shen-chuan* (The Investiture of the Gods), *Shui-hu* (Water Margin), *Ju-lin wai-shih* (The Scholars),

San-kuo yen-i (Romance of the Three Kingdoms), *Hung-lou-meng* (Dream of the Red Chamber), *Ch'i-hsia wu-i* (Seven Heroes and Five Gallants), *P'in-hua pao-chien* (Mirror of Theatrical Life), and *Erh-nü ying-hsiung chuan* (The Gallant Maid).[5] These are only representative titles; similar ones or imitations of any of them, I do not list.[6]

His literary fare did not contain anything unusual, but he adds a very interesting and unorthodox opinion on the educational value of these books:

I owe it almost completely to the reading of novels that I mastered the reading of literary Chinese. The classics were really of no assistance at all. I therefore cannot help feeling that my avid reading of novels has been very rewarding.[7]

This method of acquiring a knowledge of literary Chinese seems to have had a tradition in the Chou family since he reports of his grandfather, a *han-lin* scholar of early Kuanghsü times,[8] that when he taught his offspring literary composition, "as a first step, he would tell them to do some reading on their own, and he particularly encouraged them to read novels, as this would bring about their mastery of literary Chinese. Only after this was mastered could anything else be attempted." [9] Chou's avid reading of novels, apart from their pedagogic value, it is safe to assume, would also have further stimulated his literary bent and influenced his taste, drawing him away from the classics and more toward popular topics and toward a fluid, realistic style of prose writing.

Chou's later enrollment in a foreign-oriented, technically inclined naval academy is neither an indication of his predilections nor of any direct consequence to his literary development. It had been a step taken merely out of the necessity to find a tuition-free education.[10] The technical subjects of the academy did not hold Chou's interest. A fruitful result of his stay at the academy was that he learned English; thereby, he obtained direct access to a new world, the world of Western literature and Western thought.

The new impressions he derived from reading foreign literatures must have been very deep, because he almost immediately attempted to emulate the stories that he read in his English textbooks or in the translations of Lin Shu [11] and Yen Fu.[12] He tried his hand at translation and reproduced first *Ali Baba and the Forty Thieves* and later Edgar Allan Poe's "The Gold Bug" in

literary Chinese.[13] Under the same spell, he also attempted to
write his own novel, which he called *Ku-erh-chi* (Story of an
Orphan). In later years, Chou recalled with amusement how, for
lack of any personal creative imagination, he had to borrow heavily
and in increasing measure on the plot of Victor Hugo's *Claude
Gueux*. Chou reports on the birth of his novel as follows:

At that time, Su Man-shu was publishing a translation of *Les Miséra-
bles* in a Shanghai newspaper and Liang Ch'i-ch'ao often referred to
Hugo in the *Hsin-hsiao-shuo* (New Fiction), so that I became an
admirer of Hugo and painfully, all by myself, collected his works.
It was quite a job to get sixteen dollars together to buy an eight volume
American edition of Hugo's selected works. This was as large a set
as I had ever seen; since it was so large, I could not read more than
sections of "The Last Day of the Condemned" and "Claude Gueux,"
which I frequently leafed through. In 1906, when I lived in the
empty "Torpedo Hall," [14] I suddenly decided to write a novel. I
chose the title *Ku-erh-chi* (The Story of an Orphan) and wrote about
the life of an orphan. The first part was my own creation, making
the best of my poor imagination. But this gave out when I got to the
part where the orphan becomes a thief, and I put as much of Hugo's
material in as possible, so that in the latter part, the orphan becomes
Claude Gueux. Whether there was any statement about this in the
introduction, I don't remember anymore, as I also don't remember
what pseudonym I used. I sent this novel of about 20,000 words
directly to the *Hsiao-shuo-lin* (Forest of Fiction) magazine, where it
was accepted. I even received twenty dollars for it; this was the first
pay I ever earned.[15]

This experience must have made Chou realize once and for all that
imaginative writing was beyond the scope of his artistic capacities
and also alien to his character. As we see him engaged in his
first literary experiments, we may perhaps reflect here on the personal endowments that certainly directed his literary motivations
and also directly influenced his preference of literary genre. First
of all, we should mention his devotion to truth. From his early
studies of the classics he adopted as his favorite slogan Confucius'
dictum: "When you know a thing, to hold that you know it; and
when you do not know a thing, to allow that you do not know it;—
this is knowledge." [16] The need for a truthful and honest acknowl-
edgment of the limits of one's own knowledge was thus regarded as
an essential prerequisite of all human intellectual activity. Throughout the great changes that marked his formative years—in fact,

throughout his life—Chou maintained an imperturbable honesty of character and purpose and a devotion to truth, a truth based on common sense and reason which left no place for distorting emotionalism or traditionalism.

It is, for instance, revealing and of pertinent interest in this connection that, when reflecting on the myriads of names in China's long literary history, Chou could name only three men as being truly deserving of unqualified admiration and emulation.[17] Wang Ch'ung, Li Chih, and Yü Cheng-hsieh shared the personal traits of unswerving and unstinting honesty, combined with the courage to condemn the superstitions and other irrational evils of their time and to speak out boldly for human dignity and reason. They did so as rebels of the pen, rather than of the sword, as members of the intellectual nobility of their time, as men of culture and high ethical standards. Let us examine their outstanding characteristics singly and in more detail.

Wang Ch'ung (A.D. 27–ca. 100), the "most original and ingenious thinker among Han period philosophers," [18] is known for his pragmatic denial of the existence of ghosts and for his opposition to the diverse rituals and superstitions justified by nothing but a belief in spirits. Equally daring for his time was the deidolization of the "golden past" and its saints and sages. Wang Ch'ung's main work, the *Lun-heng* (Critical Disquisitions), has come down to us almost intact. Only one of its eighty-five chapters is missing. Most often quoted and significant of the man and his work is the phrase *Lun-heng shih-shih chi-wang* (The Lun-heng affirms facts and abhors falsehood) from the "Tui-tso-p'ien" section of the work.

Li Chih (1527–1602) was a spiritual follower of Wang Yangming (1472–1528) and his school, a movement that is compared to the Reformation in Europe. Li, at first, seemed to be progressing well in his civil service career, when he suddenly resigned to go into self-imposed exile in order to escape the restraints of official life. He voiced uncompromising opposition to traditionalism, in particular to the neo-Confucianism of his time, whenever he felt its dogma to conflict with the human conscience and the sane deductions of human reason. For instance, he is said to have admitted women to his lectures, an unheard-of procedure for his age and for many centuries to come. For his unorthodox views, he was finally thrown into prison, where he committed suicide.[19]

Yü Cheng-hsieh (1775–1840) was a scholar of wide learning.

His two main works, *Kuei-ssu lei-kao* and *Kuei-ssu ts'un-kao,* are repositories of encyclopedic information. He employed modern critical and scientific methods in such fields as historical, medical, astronomical, and geographical research. Yü voiced surprisingly advanced ideas, particularly in defense of the rights of women and against the prevailing double moral standard.[20] These short characterizations reveal why Chou Tso-jen chose these particular men to illustrate his ideals of learning and culture.

The quest for a state of reason and truth was, in essence, the basis of the new culture movement and the reason for Chou and his generation of intellectuals to reject much of the national cultural heritage, which, to their critical and sometimes hypercritical minds, failed to meet the requirements of modern life and therefore had to be discarded. On the other hand, Western civilization—known mostly through book reading only—impressed and fascinated them, as it appeared to present a lucid example of uninterrupted human progress toward reason and truth, starting with the humanism of the ancient Greeks, through the Renaissance and Enlightenment, and down to such modern seekers of truth as Spencer, Huxley, and Nietzsche.[21]

If it was then Havelock Ellis [22] whom Chou Tso-jen singled out among contemporary Western writers as deserving of highest esteem, it was because he saw Ellis as a man of enlightened thought with the personal honesty and courage to proclaim new truths in order to destroy traditional prejudices and untruth. This emphasis on truthfulness and reason by Chou Tso-jen, of course, reveals only part of his complex nature. There were, for instance, also strong elements of emotional sensitivity and romantic attachments in his nature. By way of example, we may mention his romantic love for the Shaohsing area, his native place, which always held a peculiar charm for him, even though he visited it seldom in his adult years.[23] Yet he always liked to reminisce on the days of his youth in Shaohsing, and he never ceased to collect books on the customs, folklore, and folk songs of *Yüeh,* that is, modern-day Chekiang province.

Another aspect of Chou Tso-jen's character that was certainly relevant to his literary career was his peaceable and tranquil disposition. He was not by nature a fighter; in his temperament there was nothing pugnacious or bellicose. In this respect, he displayed the nature of the true *chün-tzu,* the Confucian gentleman, despite an often expressed disdain for traditional Confucianism. He realized the fact himself when he admitted on one occasion: "My 'gentry' temperament after all is still very deep-rooted; essentially I am a man of *chung-yung* ideology." [24] The term *chung-yung* occurs frequently in Chou's writings, or writing on Chou Tso-jen, either as an adjective or noun or in the form of an ism. He frequently equates it with the Greek *sophrosyne,* a quality of "wise moderation and discreet good sense; discretion, temperance." [25] The temperance and serenity of most of his writings are indeed eloquent testimony to the *sophrosyne* trait in his character and temperament.

How do all these personal character traits relate to the essay? Why should they influence Chou Tso-jen's preference for this literary genre? The essay in its informality presupposes frankness and honesty of thought and expression, as does the essay's *Ich-Bezogenheit* (personal involvement).[26] In its informality, the language of the essay is naturally the everyday language of the people; use of the "everyday language of the people" was an evolution that Chou ardently supported. It foregoes all pretentious embellishments and has no use for prosodic fetters. The essay is basically peaceful reflection, far from bellicose diatribe; it is contemplative, not assertive. It also presupposes philosophical curiosity without exhaustiveness. It is usually characterized by a certain temperance and tranquillity. All these elements of the essay reflect one or the other of Chou Tso-jen's character traits and inclinations, and this harmonious bond between his own personality and the essential characteristics of the essay helps to explain why he felt intuitively drawn to the essay form in the first instance and why he also, to some extent at least, achieved a superb mastery of this particular literary medium.

CHAPTER 4

Stylistic Elements

T HE informal, untrammeled, and personal nature of the essay has led some to doubt its artistic value.[1] Artistic value in all forms of art will of course always remain a very subjective concept; it will depend on the artist's mode of expression and on the appreciation of such forms by whosoever evaluates them.[2] In the sphere of literature, the artist uses language to express himself; we shall, therefore, examine here the language and style of Chou Tso-jen's writings to determine their artistic qualities.

I *Language*

The question of language assumed a particular significance in China in early Republican times, as it was not only a problem of personal style but the very much larger problem of choosing between the use of the traditional literary language, the *wen-yen,* and the use of the vernacular, the *pai-hua.*[3] We have indicated previously that Chou Tso-jen was one of the early supporters of the *pai-hua* movement. It is, in fact, in this field that he made a very significant contribution to modern Chinese literary developments. His pioneering use of *pai-hua* constituted a forceful impulse to the whole movement; his ability to use the "new literary language" in a polished, artistic way provided brilliant vindication of its adequacy and artistic value, and it destroyed "the superstition that had alleged works of literature could not be written a *pai-hua.*"[4] To speak here of a "new" literary language perhaps requires explanation, since the use of the vernacular, as such, was not new in Chinese literature, but had had a very long tradition, as set forth, for instance, by Hu Shih in his *History of Pai-hua Literature.*[5]

Yet, during the period we are concerned with here, there had begun such an influx of new objects, new institutions, and new ideas into China, all exacting accommodation in the national language, that the result was a unique acceleration of language development. In view of its new form and vocabulary, we are indeed justified to speak of a "new" literary language evolving at that time. As Chou Tso-jen once expressed it: "The new things could not be pushed into the old bag. The new thought required a new form of writing for its communication; that is why *pai-hua* had to be used." [6]

That foreign influences helped mold the new literary language is undeniable. As a consequence, many neologisms and foreignisms (particularly Anglicisms) are noticeable in the writings of the early *pai-hua* proponents. Purists were quick to deplore what they considered to be a desecration of the national language.[7] However, their protests were in the end swept away by the sheer necessity of change. Chou Tso-jen felt little concern for nationalistic or esthetic matters in this situation of rapid linguistic change, as long as it served the purpose of providing an efficient vehicle for the expression of modern ideas and the description of modern things. He even tended to encourage the importation of foreign elements into the Chinese language as a means of enriching and modernizing the language, showing here again his distinctly cosmopolitan spirit, free from the narrow chauvinism of some of his contemporaries. We find him using, for instance, such expressions as "public scapegoat," "scales fell from my eyes," "to pull chestnuts from the fire," "throw out the child with the bath," and others in literal translation.[8] As an artist, however, Chou did show some esthetic reserve when he criticized the degrading of good English words in the journalese of the Shanghai press, like the use of *mo-t'e-erh* to mean "model" and then merely "girl in undress" or *ming-hsing* (star) to mean "artist" and in particular a cinema actress of doubtful repute. He also pointed critically to such Japanese monstrosities as *raburetta* for "love letter," *modan garu* for "modern girl," and the like, as unnecessary and unbearably ugly mimicking of foreign word-sounds.[9] The language problem was but one of many matters of concern during the literary reform movement, and discussion ranged over a wide field, from the need for Esperanto (in which Chou at times showed a lukewarm interest),[10] to the introduction of the feminine third-person pronoun written with the *nü* (woman) "radical" (of which he approved).[11] In all his essays on the various aspects of the language problem and in his own use of modernized and newly evolved terms, Chou showed good judgment and a sophisticated artist's good taste. He stigmatized abuse and by actual application furnished proof of the usability of the modern terms of which he approved.

If Chou acknowledged the *pai-hua* as the literary language of modern China, he was, on the other hand, not as violently antagonistic as others were toward the *wen-yen,* the traditional literary language. He objected to Hu Shih's calling *wen-yen* a dead language.[12] This indicates that he was personally still able to regard it as a living tradition. For him, it was a medium in which he was able to move about quite freely, as he was wont to demonstrate occasionally by composing old-style poetry or essays in the *wen-yen.*[13] It was also no doubt vitally important to him as the medium through which he drew nourishment from China's rich literary heritage, to which he never ceased to feel closely bound and deeply obligated. The avowedly strong foreign influences and trends toward foreignisms were never strong enough to obliterate his roots in the Chinese tradition. Even his "new" literary language always appears as the cultured expression of a Chinese well grounded in the literary tradition of his country. As a modern critic expressed it in one particular case: "The outer form . . . may carry a thick Japanese lustre, but inside the structure of the language is definitely old Chinese, with the 'spirit and marrow' of the Chinese *pi-chi* (literary notebook) essays." [14]

Chou occasionally deplored [15] what he regarded as the inadequacy of his classical literary schooling. The curriculum he completed was indeed short as compared to instruction in the complete series of classics, but his great skill in writing literary Chinese, his wide range of discerning reading,[16] and his familiarity with the Chinese literature of the past lead us to conclude that his education was profound even by traditional Chinese standards.[17] The traditional literary language, as well as the new *pai-hua,* were easily and abundantly at his disposal. He was a natural writer who needed no drafting and little correcting. "He never made out a draft before writing an article. He wrote right through at one sitting, checked only once for misspelled words, and then the article was ready." [18] There was certainly nothing labored or artificial in his manner, as we can judge from this remark by one of his close friends.

II *Style*

This leads us beyond the purely linguistic element to a consideration of Chou's style of writing. If we understand style to be the "embodiment of the writer's thoughts in words which express not only his ideas but his personality," [19] it is little wonder that we find his style of writing characterized by clarity and simplicity of diction and sentence structure. His vocabulary is comparatively simple, but to the point, and the sentences are usually short and lucid. It is significant to mention here that among the models of the past, Chou particularly admired and tried to emulate the style of Wang Ch'ung, with that writer's well-known emphatic distaste for the false and pretentious. [20]

The flow of words, sentences, and ideas is easy and smooth, just "like running water that nimbly flows along . . . allowed to meander, to go where it pleases, into minute details, but shunning exhaustion of the subject. Exhaustiveness is like a bay of dead water. Chou's writings are like a brook, a rivulet that has not yet been dyked in and can take its winding course as it pleases and without the least effort." [21] The picture of the lively brook is obviously an allusion to Chou Tso-jen's poem "Hsiao-ho" (Rivulet), generally considered to be the most accomplished of his attempts at *pai-hua* poetry. [22] Fluidity of style, which is meant here by the simile of the lively brook, is vitally essential in good essay writing because the digressiveness of the essay—in the above simile the "meandering water"—could otherwise become a strain on the reader's attention. Simplicity and clarity of style, however, do not diminish the particular mood that is so characteristic of good essay writing.

III *Mood*

As to the mood and temper characteristic of his essays, here again we find strikingly reflected the writer's own character and personality. It is both interesting and revealing to refer to the descriptions of such stylistic features as defined by some of his contemporaries. Chinese literary critics, it must be noted, are still accustomed to employ many of the time-honored phrases that have been handed down from the days of Liu Hsieh's *Wen-hsin tiao-lung* [23] and Ssu-k'ung T'u's (837–908) *Shih-p'in* (Poetic Qualities). [24] They baffle the foreign translator [25] as they are merely abstract approximations of impressions a piece of art works on the mind and the emotions stimulated in a perceptive audience, but they can be extremely expressive and meaningful in their own way. The terms most frequently used by contemporary literary critics to describe the art of Chou Tso-jen are *ch'ing-tan, p'ing-tan,* and *ch'ung-tan.*[26] The recurring "tan" denotes the purity of a liquid that has not been adulterated, spiced, or excessively flavored. *Ch'ing-tan* then seems to emphasize mildness and purity, freedom from adulterations, admixtures, or heavy one-sided flavoring. The term "p'ing-tan" has added in *p'ing* a vision of an unruffled expanse of water, while the "ch'ung" in *ch'ung-tan* conveys the idea of rinsing out all hard and harsh colors to leave behind only shades of pastel lightness.

Others, in attempting to characterize the salient qualities of his prose manner, emphasize one particular mood, as for instance the idyllic, the nearness to nature and aloofness from human toil and struggle, as in the following description:

Reading [Chou's] essays is like suddenly finding oneself on the road to the Western Hills after a long stay in the city of Peking. The songs of the birds evoke a consciousness of Spring. One blade of grass, a little pond, can stir a love of nature. The sound of a frog as it jumps into the water conveys a sense of motion and stillness. The waving pines and the murmur of springs bring a realization of beauty. On returning to the city, hateful will be the hustle and bustle, the villainy of man towards man, the injustice of punishments and rewards, the senseless bonds of antiquated customs! What a marvellous trip it had been, there was solitary seclusion, there will be a rebellious spirit! [27]

The "frog jumping into the water" seems to be an allusion to the famous *haiku* poem of Matsuō Bashō (1644–94): "The old pond! A frog jumps in—Sound of the water." [28] Chou Tso-jen was very fond of this type of poetry. The "solitary seclusion" and "rebellious spirit" seem to allude to the "Rebel and Recluse," that is, I. Goldberg's characterization of Havelock Ellis,[29] which characterization Chou Tso-jen very much wanted to apply to himself, too.[30] The above characterization of the mood of his essays reminds us also of Lin Yutang's similar statement on the essay mood: "The mind recaptures the freedom which it had lost during the hustle and bustle of the day." [31] On at least one occasion, Chou himself professed that he was actively aiming at what he called the tranquil, unconcerned, natural style that he admired so much in certain

Chinese and Western writers, but which, as he says in self-depre-
cating modesty, he could not even "dream of achieving himself." [32]

Also indicative of the mood and sentiment of his essays are
many of the titles and subtitles that he chose for his collections,
sometimes adding his own interpretations of such titles to leave no
doubt as to their significance. The title *Yü-t'ien ti shu* (A Rainy
Day's Book) is meant to suggest the depressing atmosphere of
dark clouds and dampness, but: "At such times I used to imagine
myself in a little hut in a riverside village, sitting next to the
window and feeling the warmth of a charcoal brazier, and chatting
with a friend over a cup of tea. What cozy happiness." [33] The title
K'an-yün-chi (Looking-at-Clouds Anthology) conveys a mood of
leisurely, contemplative reverie, and this is confirmed when Chou
explains [34] that the title is a quotation from a poem by Wang Wei:
"walking up to where the brook ends and sitting there looking at
the clouds rising." [35]

To the first anthology of his essays published in China, Chou
gave the title *Tzu-chi ti yüan-ti* (One's Own Garden), which to a
Chinese reader will no doubt bring to mind T'ao Yüan-ming and
his withdrawal from the mundane world to the idyllic, untrammeled
life of a gardener. (The title, though, is actually a quotation from
Voltaire.[36]) One subsection of the above-mentioned anthology is
entitled *Ch'a-hua* (Tea Chat), which is explained by Chou himself, rather significantly, as follows:

"Tea chat" literally means chatting while drinking tea, but actually I
have hardly ever chatted this way; besides, I am not a connoisseur of
tea—I merely drink cold tea like a fish drinks water. The heading
"Tea Chat" shall only indicate that these are clear, calm, and unconcerned talks, as one would chat over a cup of tea, and not the muddled,
heavy talk after wine.[37]

Though perhaps not a connoisseur of tea, Chou, nonetheless,
appreciated tea drinking as an enjoyable, leisurely relaxation, and
recommended it in the following, oft-quoted remark:

Tea should be had in a place with a tiled roof and papered windows,
using water from a pure spring, with green tea, in simple elegant
porcelain utensils, in the company of two or three others. Half a day
of such relaxation is worth ten years in this world of toil.[38]

The essay in which this passage occurs is indeed so illustrative of
Chou's mood of unconcern and relaxed philosophy of life that I

have thought it worth an attempt at translation (see "Tea Drinking" in Chapter 5 below). The larger part of his essays reflects the same mood of cool reserve and gentle aloofness, even at such times as when he joins in discussions on social and political questions and chooses to take a definite stand on controversies of the day. This manner of emotional restraint was the more conspicuous as it often strongly contrasted with the passionate revolutionary temper of the time.

What is sometimes taken to be a mood of aloofness may also often merely be a reflection of his attempt to delineate underlying causes of social phenomena rather than obvious and provocative symptoms. One instance of this kind was a public debate on Yü Ta-fu's (1896–1945) novel *Ch'en-lun* (Sinking),[39] which had become the subject of much controversy because of its "preoccupation with sexual fantasies." [40] Entering the debate, Chou avoided vulgar polemics and moved the argument to a higher level of objective consideration of basic social and moral concepts. As another instance, we may perhaps refer to his effort to introduce the ideas of such writers as Edward Carpenter [41] and Havelock Ellis to his contemporaries, his purposes being to attempt to change popular attitudes toward such matters as respect for womanhood and mutuality and dignity in relationships between the sexes.

In spite of a semblance of outward simplicity, Chou's essays are not without great depth and sophistication of thought, which may at times have engendered in contemporary readers an impression of aloofness and unconcern. Fond of quoting writers of the past, he also often tried to prove that many ideas hailed as revolutionary and new were actually nothing but the rediscovered wisdom of antiquity. Frequent digressions into the past, no matter how pertinent, also contributed to the impression of withdrawal and remoteness. The same effect often resulted from a bent for introducing elements of foreign art and culture. In this respect, it was not so much the immediate and practical, but rather the deeper humanitarian and esthetic, values of foreign cultures that held his attention and that he wrote about. There is, for instance, the large number of essays in which he tried to acquaint his countrymen with various laudable aspects of the culture of Japan, in seeming disregard of the fact that his country was, for all practical purposes, at war with Japan.

In this connection, we may perhaps refer also to his persistent esthetic sensitivity, the true artist's enjoyment of esthetic creation for its own sake. Very often this unconcern for the mundane, the purposeful, conveys an impression of aloofness. His veneration of Greek mythology and of the folk and fairy tales of peoples completely alien to his reading public bear signs of this attitude. Although he disavowed "art for art's sake" as a valid principle of literary philosophy, yet in actual fact many of his essays come very near to being impressionistic mood paintings or digress into purely esthetic contemplation. Good examples are the "Hsi-shan hsiao-p'in" (Essays from the Western Hills),[42] two narrative essays describing life at a temple resort in the Western Hills near Peking, where Chou retreated to recuperate from an illness. Descriptions of the peaceful scenery of the Western Hills, and the restful leisure of convalescence impart a mood of tranquillity and remoteness, a mood which is frequently encountered in many of his essays.

Earlier attempts at a type of symbolistic poetry, which he called *san-wen-shih* (poetical essays),[43] like "Hsiao-ho" (Rivulet), "Ch'i-lu" (Crossroads), "Ts'ang-ying" (Flies), should be mentioned in this context. In the foreword to "Hsiao-ho," which was first published in the magazine *Hsin-ch'ing-nien* (New Youth), Chou acknowledged the influence of Baudelaire, the pioneer of modern symbolism, and underlined the affinity by translating two of Baudelaire's poems, namely "L'Étranger" and "Les Fenêtres," into Chinese.[44] Significant, too, are other foreign writings he selected for translation; for instance, the works of the estheticist and symbolist Remy de Gourmont, or the imitation of Christina Rossetti's *Goblin Market* in his "Kuei ti chiao-mai" (The Goblin Street-Vendor's Call).

The manifestation of an aloof, serene, or remote manner was not always apt to evoke an appreciative applause from the reading public. The reaction of many of his readers, less endowed with a bent for esthetic contemplation, or unable, due to the turmoils of the time, to muster his peace of mind or delight in the purposeless, can well be imagined to have been one of vexation at his "indifference" toward burning questions of the day. An essay written and published only seven months after the Lukouch'iao incident of 1937 took as its subject "Speaking of Candy Selling." [45] For these reasons, some decried the whole genre of the personal or familiar essay as a "narcotic," a "little ornament," or an "amusement during tea or after wine." [46]

IX *Humor*

Another element in the essays of Chou Tso-jen that can be discussed as a mood or stylistic technique is that of humor. Humor can differ in form and in meaning, from a semantic seasoning to a deep philosophical purport, from an expression of happiness to an instrument of resentment and hate. Here again, the author's temperament and philosophy of life will determine which type will predominate in his works. A master of the vernacular, Chou Tso-jen made frequent and consistent use of humorous elements present in the language of the common people. Although he never achieved a sense of local color and flavor, as did Lao She,[47] for instance, in his novels, many idiomatic phrases, popular metaphors, the so-called *ch'eng-yü,* and humorous folk tales enrich his writings. A typical, humorous anecdote retold in an essay goes as follows: "A man told to cut off a limb as the only way to cure his father, goes instead into the street and cuts off a beggar's leg. To the wailing beggar he remonstrates: Hush, don't complain, this is practicing filial piety!" [48]

In his essays on social and political questions, Chou tends toward witty satire, not as aggressive and biting as that employed by his brother Lu Hsün, but of a more temperate and intellectual type, and frequently following the traditional Chinese practice of alluding to older or classical writings. Humor in his essays is generally not the humor of jocular phrases or comic situations however, but rather the pervading mood of "good humor," the expression of harmony and happiness, gained by a person of a well-adjusted and understanding mentality. It is not a loudly extrovert hilarity but rather a "quietistic humor," [49] the perceptive observation and gentle exposure of human vanities and foibles, with the somewhat superior smile of a more knowledgeable person.

True to his conviction that the natural disposition of man is good, that the emotions have their proper function in life, and that they, therefore, deserve a place in the general scheme of things, he also thought of humor as a natural endowment that should be nurtured and practiced, and of which, in fact, there could never be enough, provided it was properly presented and well taken.[50] He was gratified to find a rich native tradition of humorous literature and demonstrated his support for humor by collecting and publishing an anthology, the *K'u-ch'a-an hsiao-hua hsüan* (Collection of Humorous Tales from the "Bitter Tea" Hermitage). Chou also introduced some specimens of foreign humor, namely the humor of the Japanese *kyogen* plays—the comic interludes of *nō* performances [51]—as well as the satire of Jonathan Swift,[52] to the Chinese reading public. Judging by the native and foreign humor he selected to translate or anthologize, he preferred a more restrained, subdued, and witty type of humor, as is usually thought characteristic of the Japanese and the British, rather than extrovert clowning or boisterous display.[53]

CHAPTER 5

Analysis of the Essays

CHOU Tso-jen's interests can indeed be described as all-encompassing and cosmopolitan, and the range of subjects treated in his writings over the years is, therefore, extremely wide. To group his essays by subject matter types—though not impossible —would serve relatively little purpose. This has been attempted, and in an introduction to the *Chou Tso-jen hsüan-chi* (The Selected Works of Chou Tso-jen), the editors distinguish four types of essays: (a) on literary art and other treatises; (b) book reviews, prefaces, and postscripts; (c) short stories and familiar essays; and (d) vignettes of life. In the Preface to *Hsiao-p'in-wen chiang-hua* (Lectures on the Casual Essay), the critic Shih Wei suggests the following classification: (a) description of scenery, (b) description of things, (c) narrative essays, (d) lyrical essays, (e) reveries, (f) treatises on serious subjects, and (g) satire. As varied topically as the essay may be, there is little doubt that specimens of each class indicated above can be found among the essays of Chou Tso-jen. In a 1945 survey [1] of his own writings, Chou divided the immense corpus of his essays into two simple and basic types: (1) *cheng-ching,* serious, or purposeful essays; and (2) *hsien-shih,* essays of leisure and one's own fancy.[2]

The following analysis will proceed in a somewhat chronological and geographical order; that is to say, the times and places where creative impulses occurred, or may be presumed to have occurred, will serve as points of reference, though, obviously, impressions often linger on and stimulate literary expression much later than during the phase of initial contact.

32

I *Early Impressions—Shaohsing, Nanking, Peking*

The early years passed at Shaohsing, the place and its customs, the home and his family, are frequent topics of essays of reminiscence. Mostly autobiographical or concerned with his brother's early youth, these essays were written off and on throughout his literary career. They display a strong attachment for his native place and a vivid memory of his experiences there.

As a cadet at the Naval Academy in Nanking, Chou Tso-jen first turned his hand to prose writing, as has been indicated above,[3] but these initial literary ventures do not belong to the essay proper. This particular period in his life did not otherwise inspire much reminiscence in later years, except the occasional joking reference to his having started out to become a "sailor." His trip to Peking in 1905, however, left him with a rather singular lifelong impression, namely, an emphatic dislike for the Peking Opera. He recalls these experiences in an essay written in 1936 on the amenities and vexations of life in Peking.[4] The Peking Opera is of course for him one of the latter; the widespread use by 1936 of loudspeakers gave rise to the incessant broadcasting of opera music at high volume from shops, restaurants, and market places all over town. Again, as late as 1954, Chou recounts the 1905 experience in almost the same terms used in his earlier (1936) essay;[5] this time, however, he elaborates on the reasons for his negative attitude.[6] These remarks reflect to some extent the influence of the changed political environment, but they are still worth summarizing here. The ideological content of Peking Opera, he observes, is low and backward-looking; most plays perpetuate the decadent spirit of the old society in glorifying wealth, the holding of high government office, and the possession of concubines as worthy ambitions. The bearing and movements of actors on stage are inartistic and unrealistic. The music seems to be closely linked to the stilted and antiquated *pa-ku* style of writing. In its "deafening" effect, it reminds him of an evil with similar effects, namely, opium.[7]

II *Chou Tso-jen in Japan*

When Chou Tso-jen arrived in Japan in 1906, it must have seemed to him as if he were entering a new world. Visible evidence of the kinship of the Japanese and Chinese cultures, the result of centuries of contact and borrowing, was vanishing as elements of Western civilization were being assimilated much more rapidly in Japan than in China. The new arrival therefore had to cope with the problem of learning about both traditional and modern Japan, and also with the problem of absorbing the imported Western culture that had become part of the Japanese intellectual scene. At that time, Japan was also a hotbed of Chinese revolutionary activities, which was later to influence importantly political and social changes in China itself. In trying to assess the variety of influences that Chou was exposed to during his stay in Japan, influences which later manifested themselves in his essays, it is necessary to recognize that these influences were complex and only partly Japanese. To a very considerable extent he was subject to social and cultural influences emanating from Europe, and to some extent those resulting from the presence of Chinese political refugees in Japan.

III *Japanese Influences*

Chou Tso-jen arrived in Japan shortly after the Japanese military victory over Russia. At that time, the success of the Japanese Restoration and the defeat of Russia were naturally two things that appeared to every Chinese student in Japan as most impressive achievements, as Chou also recalls in his essays "Liu-hsüeh ti hui-i" (Memories of Studies Abroad). There is no doubt that he too came to admire the unique synthesis of East and West that Japan had so skillfully brought about during the Meiji period and that had resulted—among other things—in her military prowess and newly elevated status among the nations of the world. However, knowing well how little Chou was interested in politics generally, it is safe to assume that it was not Japanese political successes, nor her brilliant rise to power that made the deepest and most permanent impressions on Chou. In fact, later, at a time when militarism was about to overshadow all other aspects of Japanese life, he stated very distinctly that the true value of Japanese culture, as he had come to know and to admire it, lay somewhere else. In 1920 he wrote: "We do acknowledge that a country's glory lies in its culture—its knowledge, art, and litera- ture, and not at all in territory, power, and military strength;

these at times may even implicate and destroy its true glory." [8]
The thought that "a country's glory lies in its culture" is the key
to Chou Tso-jen's admiration of Japan. It is the theme that
permeates all of his numerous essays on things Japanese. Not the
superficial westernization in military or technical fields—no matter
how successful—but rather the deeper cultural values, meaning
in particular certain traditional traits in the character of her people
and the traditional literature and art of Japan, made him a lifelong
friend and admirer of that country.

Chou's impressions of Japan during his student years were
limited to Tokyo and its environs.[9] In time, Tokyo became a place
whose special, congenial atmosphere permitted him to feel at
home. He was later to observe:

When we went abroad to study, not understanding one word of the
foreign language, and stepped all alone into the metropolis of a foreign country, we could easily have felt forlorn and miserable. But
it was not that way with me. After only a short while, the atmosphere
of the place, at that particular time, felt harmonious and congenial, and
furthermore very likeable. If I therefore came to call Tokyo my
second home, it was a sign of my great attachment.[10]

He ascribed his ease of acclimatizing to Japanese city life partly
to similarities between life in Tokyo and Shaohsing where he had
grown up:

I grew up in a "water-community" in South-east (China). People
there live frugal and hard lives. In winter the houses have no heating
and cold winds blow right into one's bedcovers. Throughout the year
we have always had very salty pickled vegetables or very salty
pickled fish. Brought up in this way, one will find nothing inconvenient
when going to live in Tokyo.[11]

From the beginning, Chou adopted a Japanese style of living
and eating, and, although the need to economize may also have
had something to do with it, he came to like it. "I am fond of
Japanese houses for the same reason that I like their food; they
are simple and suited to a simple way of life," he wrote.[12] In many
aspects of Japanese life, Chou and his compatriots were happy to
recognize elements of old Chinese culture, which had been
adopted and adapted by the Japanese. For instance, the wearing
of the Japanese kimono was considered not only a convenience
but also a patriotic gesture at that time, since the kimono

resembled Chinese native dress as worn before the Manchus imposed their "barbarian" customs on the Chinese:

We thought we could very well wear Japanese native-style dress. Since the *p'ao-tzu* and *ma-kua* (Chinese men's wear of Manchu origin) were held to be barbarian clothes in pre-Ch'ing dynasty times, it would indeed have amounted to expressing subservience (to the Manchus) to wear them in Tokyo.[13]

Similar experiences in Tokyo are expressed in another essay, as follows:

I lived uninterruptedly for only six years in Tokyo, but I grew very fond of the place, and feel about it as if it were my second home. . . . Why? Tokyo's climate cannot compare with Peking's; there is a continuous threat of earthquakes and fires. We also had no money to spare for tours of the scenic spots and historic places—as students on government scholarship, you can easily imagine our position— and amusements were of course out of the question. However, I liked the Japanese way of life in Tokyo, meaning thereby traditional Japanese clothes, food, and houses.[14]

Although one might consider his adoption of Japanese style living merely as an outward adaption to circumstances, it does however, seem to have had a more meaningful significance for him. He appreciated the congeniality and artistic life style of the Japanese people and his attitude reflected a sincere desire to experience and understand better the life of the people among whom he had come to live. In an old style poem that he must have penned shortly before leaving Japan in 1912, Chou expressed his feelings in this way: "I travelled far, yet do not yearn for home. By long sojourn, I love this once-strange place." [15]

Chou Tso-jen indeed came to admire much in the native customs of the Japanese, much of what might be called their national character, and this admiration is expressed in the following lines from one of his essays:

There are also certain customs in the Japanese way of life that I like; for instance, their cleanliness, their politeness, and their untrammeled naturalness. "Untrammeled naturalness" seems at first to conflict with "politeness," but actually that is not so. It is not a coarse vulgarity, but merely the absence of false morality or religious and Taoist teachings, and the absence of the mock-proprieties that are born of lewdness and idleness.[16]

Chou claimed that China also had had this "untrammeled naturalness," particularly under the T'ang dynasty, but that neo-Confucianism, with its stringent dogmas and many social taboos, had later eradicated it in China. In Japan, however, these emanations of T'ang culture managed to persist. After contributing abundantly to the great flowering of culture in the Heian period (A.D. 800–1186), they had become so strongly established that whatever neo-Confucian influences did reach Japan could not dislodge the heritage of T'ang-Heian cultural patterns.[17]

Among the character traits of the Japanese people, it was particularly their emotional sensitivity that impressed him and which, in some way, he tried to emulate. In his later years, he once reflected: "The miscellany of my learning I owe to a great extent to foreign influences through the medium of English and Japanese literature. I could analyse it here in this way: what pertains to knowledge, I generally obtained from the West, what pertains to the emotional, I mostly derived from Japan." [18] To understand this remark fully, it is necessary to remember that European culture, to the extent that Chou had been exposed to it before arriving in Japan, consisted mainly of elements of science and philosophy, and particularly the mathematics that he had had to study at school and the Western philosophy and logic that he had imbibed in the translations of Yen Fu.[19] Even the belletristic translations of Lin Shu,[20] which he had read with great enthusiasm, as he admits, must have appealed more to his intellect than to his emotions because of their alien form and content, their European background and mentality. Japanese literature, on the other hand, with its strong emotional and lyrical ingredients—all set in an environment that was becoming more and more familiar through direct personal experience and that presented itself in the familiar script of his own cultural tradition—evoked an immediate response.[21] It became a homestead for his soul to rest and delight in, after toiling in the world of reason and purpose of his Western studies.

The Japanese intellectual life which Chou increasingly came to share, to the degree that he perfected his knowledge of Japanese, was at that time in a most active and promising stage of evolution and was comparatively free from the governmental interferences of later years. The seeds planted by Japan's great pioneers of European-style Enlightenment, like Fukuzawa Yukichi [22] and

Futabatei Shimei,[23] were in full flower. A short period of reaction
by nationalistic idealists had just about run its course, and a more
sophisticated modernism, emphasizing individualism and humanitarianism, nourished literary works of a surprising variety and
accomplishment.[24] To Chou Tso-jen, the works of contemporary
Japanese novelists and essayists provided a source of personal
inspiration: "The Japanese novel has made astounding progress
during the twentieth century. It is not only a glorious achievement
as a national literature, but many of its eminent works have
universal value and can compare with modern European literature." [25]

In one of his first lectures in Peking—at the Literary Research
Institute of Peking University—Chou elaborated this point of view,
at the same time revealing a remarkable familiarity with all phases
of contemporary Japanese prose literature.[26] During the many
years that followed, when he occupied the chair of Japanese
literature at Peking University, his knowledge of the subject and
his appreciation of Japanese culture in general continued to deepen.
Numerous essays on Japanese customs and culture came from his
pen, and all reveal a warmth of understanding and admiring
sympathy which he tried to impart to his countrymen, sometimes
under the most adverse of political circumstances.

IV Western Influences

The main subject of Chou Tso-jen's studies in Japan was
European literature. An essay reminiscing about his early years
in Tokyo contains the following intimate and fairly detailed account of his motivations at that time:

The foreign language that I learned at the Naval Academy in Nanking
was English. At that time I was specializing in marine engineering.
Later the Office in Charge of [Overseas] Trainees [27] ordered me to
change to civil engineering; however, my own interests were in literature. It was therefore quite common for me to get myself a few books
to study the history of English literature. Actually, it was not only
that English has always been a means to an end for me. It certainly
enabled me as well to become acquainted with the beauty and abundance of English prose writings in the eighteenth century and thereafter, as, for instance, [the writings of] Addison, Swift, Lamb, Stevenson, Milne, and Lynd, whose essays I like to read even to this day;
but all that time my ambition was directed towards the so-called

continental literature, or the literature of weak, small nations. I used English only as my intermediary to transmit communications, much like a marriage go-between.[28]

His concern for the literature of the "weak and small" nations of Europe was—as has been mentioned in his biography and which will be further elucidated in a later paragraph—primarily the result of Chinese nationalist influences. Here it is necessary only to take note of the list of English prose writers—and there may have been many others of the same category—who had a deep and lasting influence on him. Those essayists he mentions specifically in the above quotation, all early nineteenth-century English writers, represented models to emulate.

However, apart from essayists, there was yet another and, in the long run, more important discovery to be made in English literature and scholarship. Still in this early period of literary study, Chou Tso-jen discovered Havelock Ellis. The influence of Havelock Ellis was to affect his whole philosophy and thinking on life, art, and society in general; the writings of Ellis also were to appear as direct quotations or as a latent source of inspiration in innumerable essays. He describes that discovery as follows:

Lastly and most important was [the purchase of] Ellis' *Studies in the Psychology of Sex* in seven volumes; that was the book of my enlightenment. When reading this book it was as if scales fell from my eyes and I reached a certain understanding of human life and society. In their pursuit of art, men of old frequently had sudden revelations brought about by a particular event, as also happens in the pursuit of the *tao*. A person may still be a novice at writing when a snake on the road, or a frog that leaps out from under a willow branch in the rain, may suddenly bring about his consciousness [of art].[29]

Once enlightened, Chou remained a faithful disciple. He always acknowledged his indebtedness to Havelock Ellis. For instance, in a short autobiographical note that he once wrote in the third person: "Of all books that he [Chou Tso-jen] read, those that had the greatest influence on him were the writings of the Englishman Havelock Ellis." [30]

By the time Chou discovered Ellis, the British writer and scientist was already well known in Europe, where he had gained a circle of devoted friends and admirers, as well as strong opposition from late Victorian, puritanical traditionalists. Ellis was a literary man, a medical scholar, and a humanitarian philosopher with a special interest in social, individual, and sex psychology. Although we might feel today that his literary style as well as his psychological insights are passé, there is no doubt that his writings represent pioneering achievements in the fields of psychology and philosophy.

Chou Tso-jen seems to have fallen completely under his spell right from the start,[31] and it is easy to see the reasons for this. In Ellis' works we find an admirable blending of scientific investigation and artistic expression, and a bold humanitarian message motivated by a strong interest in and sympathy for man, the individual, and for his aspirations for happiness. These, indeed, were the very ideals that were taking shape in the mind of Chou Tso-jen at that time. They were forcefully stimulated by the reading of Ellis' writings, and they were ideals for which Chou Tso-jen henceforth became an articulate spokesman in Chinese society. In the above-quoted essay, Chou states that Ellis' book on sex psychology was the first of his books that he bought and that it immediately impressed him with its scientific and yet humane and sympathetic treatment of a subject that society had so far shunned and refused to treat realistically. Henceforth, the subject of sex, the need for a new approach to sexual mores, chastity, widowhood, and the social status of women became recurring topics of his essays. Obviously, these essays were written in emulation of his great model, Havelock Ellis, so much so that he came to be called by his contemporaries the "Chinese Ellis." [32] The way that people later aproached him on such questions as sex education at Nankai Middle School,[33] or for material for a thesis on the *jus primae noctis*,[34] shows that his reputation for a broad scholarly knowledge of the subject had spread far.

Other authors whose names appear in Chou's essays on the relations of the sexes, and who also influenced him in this respect, are Edward Carpenter,[35] a close friend of Ellis, and Marie Stopes.[36] In the case of Carpenter, the demand for equality of the sexes is deemed dependent on political change. Chou rather naïvely echoes the contention that true equality will be possible only under communism, for only then, as he believed at that time, would the state assume full support of the woman during the pre- and postnatal periods, thereby ending their economic dependence on the male, the cause of their inequality.[37]

However, in his time—and in his influence on Chou Tso-jen—Ellis represented a much wider intellectual force than merely that of the "sage of sex." [38] In his affirmation of sex as the central problem of life in the General Preface to *Studies in the Psychology of Sex,* Ellis allots it a place in a general, wider scheme, which can only be described as a humane way of life. "Sex lies at the root of life, and we can never learn to reverence life until we know how to understand sex." Ellis sees life as the summation of art; or, expressed from the viewpoint of art, the supreme art is the art of living. This art man can master only if he knows the true facts of nature, only if he realizes how freedom, as well as restraint and austerity, are all inherent in nature and must be accepted by man. Finally, man must fully comprehend the unity in himself of the flesh and the spirit, the material and the spiritual. Chou Tso-jen followed Ellis in molding his own ideas on life and society. Chou emphasized the basic need to acquire a realistic knowledge of the facts of nature, as far as man is concerned, not to focus in the traditional Chinese way merely on codes of moral conduct, nor to urge upon man exertions toward inhuman and irrational perfection and saintliness, but rather to realize man's biological heritage and composition.[39] Only on the basis of this knowledge, he argued, will man be able to nurture and perfect all his potentialities, the physical as well as the spiritual, and thus achieve true inner harmony, the highest measure of human happiness, the highest artistry of life. These are the basic tenets of Ellis' philosophy, and these are also the ideas that Chou Tso-jen formulates in his essay "Humane Literature," which, being an important manifesto of his beliefs, I have translated fully (see Appendix).

The discovery of Ellis during Chou's student years in Japan is but one indication of the extent to which European rather than Japanese influences were responsible for molding his philosophy of life. Besides Ellis, many other lasting influences were derived from his English reading in Tokyo. Regarding the philosophical works of W. A. Westermarck, a follower of Spencer and a proponent of ethical relativism, Chou explicitly affirms: "His work, the *Origin and the Development of the Moral Idea,* has made a very deep impression on me." [40] *The Golden Bough* and other works by J. G. Frazer, as well as *Primitive Culture* by E. B. Taylor, provided new impulses to investigate the fields of cultural anthropology and mythology.⁴¹ Chou was also much impressed, and later tried to emulate, the mixture of scientific knowledge and literary skill that he found in the works of Andrew Lang.⁴²

A rather unusual facet of Chou Tso-jen's early literary interests is his study of Greek antiquity. The initial motivation to venture into what must have been a somewhat remote field of knowledge for a Chinese student of that time was his desire to produce a more faithful Chinese translation of the New Testament.⁴³ He later abandoned the idea, convinced that translations already in existence would be difficult to improve upon,⁴⁴ but his interest in ancient Greece, once awakened, grew into a major preoccupation. He discovered to his great delight the abundance and beauty of Greek mythology, and mythology in general was a topic of which he never tired. While a multitude of diverse interests were taken up and later dropped, as he was moved by a whim of the moment, he said:

However, there is one thing I have never tired of, have never discarded, something that seems to link together my diverse interests, and that is the study of myths. The first novel that I translated was *The World's Desire* by H. R. Haggard and Andrew Lang [London, 1890], since I had been stimulated, both by Lin Shu's translation of Haggard's adventure stories and the writings of Lang. In the Tokyo bookstores I bought such "Silver Library" books as *Custom and Myth* [London, 1884] and *Myth, Ritual, and Religion* [London, 1887], and I acquired some knowledge of the anthropological interpretation of myths. I became deeply interested in myths, and this feeling has never changed throughout these twenty years. I cannot say what my profession is, even though I am teaching now, but I can say my interest is Greek myths, because they are the most beautiful in the world.⁴⁵

This "twenty years" of preoccupation with mythology was finally to become one of sixty years' duration. Much of the time during his last years in Peking was devoted to translating from the ancient Greek.

There were no doubt still deeper reasons for his great love of ancient Greek myth. Beyond the initial motivation that led him to a study of ancient Greece, and beyond a "mundane" interest in Greek myths and folk tales, there also developed in him a deep spiritual affinity for Greek culture generally, which finally assumed greater significance than the many-splendored stories from Greek history and mythology as such. The force that attracted him more and more in this direction must be regarded as the spirit of Greek culture. In essence, the cultural ideal of ancient Greece was a harmonious blending of the sensual and the spiritual elements in man. It aimed to educate man into a human being in whom all natural potentialities might be perfected, so that ultimately life, beauty, and art would become synonymous and man would be all three in one.[46] These ideals were adopted and carried on by the Romans, who coined the word *humanitas* for them. *Humanitas,* or humanitarianism, was the only "religion" to which Chou Tso-jen admitted, a religion to which he remained faithful throughout his life. It proved to be a sustaining and reassuring source of comfort, particularly in hours of tribulation, as, for instance, during the last decades of his life under communism. It is safe to assume that it was the congenial spirit of *humanitas* which provided the deep and lasting attraction for Chou in his continuous preoccupation with the culture of ancient Greece.

V *Chinese Influences*

The Chinese living in Tokyo around the turn of the century included many political refugees, reformers, and revolutionaries who had fled there, especially after the failure of the Reform Movement of 1898. Chou particularly mentions Liang Ch'i-ch'ao [47] and Chang T'ai-yen,[48] both men of great learning and nationalist fervor. While Liang occupied himself almost exclusively with political writing and publishing during his exile in Japan, Chang devoted part of his time to lecturing to the Chinese student community on traditional Chinese culture. Chou Tso-jen had started to read Liang's writings long before he arrived in Japan and ascribed to them a strong influence on himself,[49] as was the case at that time with most youths and intellectuals throughout China. Chang T'ai-yen, on the other hand, figures much more prominently in Chou's reminiscences as a personal acquaintance and particularly as a teacher, since Chou had once belonged to a small circle of students to whom Chang T'ai-yen lectured on the *Shuo-wen,* the classic of Chinese etymology.[50]

If contacts with refugee nationalists did not draw Chou into active politics, they certainly enhanced his national consciousness and strengthened his bonds with the Chinese tradition. He later ascribed to modern Chinese nationalism certain influences that channeled his early literary interests; for instance:

At that time, Japan had men like Hasegawa Futabatei and Nobori Shōmu [51] who specialized in translations from the Russian, and Baba Kochō,[52] who introduced a volume of Continental literature. We were particularly interested in these translations, on the one hand because the *Min-pao* [53] was being published in Tokyo and the Chinese revolutionary movement was growing rapidly. We were also being influenced by the spirit of nationalism and showed greater respect and affection for the literature of the so-called despoiled and humiliated peoples, rather than of the strong countries. Among these [suffering] nations, Poland, Finland, Hungary, and modern Greece were the most important. Russia, at that time struggling against tyranny, although not weak, was also included [in our interests].[54]

The same theme recurs later in the same treatise in a more personal version:

I was originally studying for a naval career and therefore, at the start, had little opportunity to get acquainted with literature. Later, because of my enthusiasm for questions of national revolution, I attended Chang T'ai-yen's lectures. At that time Chang was inciting to action against the Manchus; that was also the reason why he lectured. Since my mind became directed towards literature of national revolution, I drew closer to the literature of the weak, small nations. As I read all kinds of works from peoples such as the Poles, the Finns, the Jews, the Indians, and others, some describing the decadent conditions in their countries, some the sorrow and pain of nations that had lost their independence, I gained a great variety of impressions and read them with great pleasure. My interest later expanded beyond the weak, small nations; I gave attention to literary works from strong countries, curious to learn what they were like. After that, I gradually broadened the sphere of my interests.[55]

It is interesting and characteristic of Chou Tso-jen's temperament and inclinations that this strong upsurge of nationalism, which stirred the Chinese refugee community in Japan at that time, led in his own case to concrete consequences mainly in the literary field. These influences appear to have intensified in him an already latent fascination for popular tales and myths, which worked to broaden his interests to include the popular literary treasures of other foreign peoples. In these endeavors, Chou acknowledges that English translations of various European works by R. Nisbet Bain [56] were a great help and source of encouragement. They drew him deeper and deeper into literary studies; without them, he once wrote: "Who knows, I may have become some local military or law officer or such, somewhere." [57]

VI   *Chou Tso-jen after His Return to China*

The overthrow of the Manchu dynasty and the establishment of a republic in China was for Chou, as for many of his fellow countrymen abroad, a call to return and to take part in the building of China into a modern state. During the initial period after his return to China in 1912, Chou's personal problems—the search for a suitable occupation and the relocation of his family—left little time or energy for writing. Consequently, few publications date from these years.[58] However, as soon as he established contact with the national intellectual life; namely, after he joined the circle of literary reformers at the National Peking University in 1917, Chou Tso-jen became more and more involved in the political and social controversies of the day and was tempted to voice his own personal views. He aligned himself with the forces of progress, and in the so-called New Literature Movement, called by some a "revolution," [59] Chou held a conspicuous position, not only as a creative writer, but also as a critic and literary theoretician.

The New Literature Movement sought to replace the formal, classical style of Chinese writing with one based on the colloquial language; but it also fostered a general reform and rejuvenation of the Chinese social and cultural life as a whole.[60] Vigorously propounding these new ideas in his writings, Chou concerned himself with a wide field of questions, from problems of social structure and relations to matters of ethics and religion. One of the basic and important questions of the day was a reevaluation of China's social and cultural tradition, which in many respects had shown itself incapable of coping with the impact of the materially superior Western civilization. The problem was not new; it had been argued by the older generation of K'ang Yu-wei [61] and Liang Ch'i-ch'ao; in a way, the abolition of the Manchu regime was a visible sign of achievement in the direction toward modernization and progress. However, in actual fact the change from an imperial to a republican regime was more symbolic than real, and the forces of tradition remained strong in the political and social field.

VII *Political Issues*

On the political stage, warlords ruled large sections of the country and continued in the footsteps of the imperial autocrats. Although emotionally and intellectually involved in the political affairs of his country, by character and temperament Chou Tso-jen was neither a revolutionary nor a politician. The political life of the times, which often seemed to constitute little more than chicanery, deceit, and personal greed, was highly distasteful to him, and direct participation in political activities conflicted with his sense of frankness and honesty and with his character and belief in decency and reason. Relatively few of his essays from this early period of the Republic, therefore, may be regarded as essentially political in nature. The most frequently quoted and best known of his political essays—in a way also the most typical in form and mood—is "P'eng shang" (Getting Oneself Hurt) (see Appendix).[62] Not an overt political pronouncement, it is rather a satirical sketch with incidental musings and is almost too witty and too detached for the cruel occasion that motivated its writing. It deals with a case of police brutality against public demonstrators and with the cynical police report that added insult to injury by blaming the people for "getting themselves hurt."

Another somewhat similar essay of that time is his "Ch'ien-men yü ma-tui chi" (An Encounter with Cavalry at the Ch'ien-men Gate).[63] On the surface, there is little political implication. A group of peaceful, harmless citizens, the author among them, are driven off some street in Peking, without any apparent reason, by a body of cavalrymen. Chou ponders the unreasonableness and impropriety of this police action, making the scene at times appear rather ludicrous and comical. His account of the incident contains nonetheless deep political meaning, a meaning that is revealed only to the more sensitive and contemplative reader. It is the tragic disregard and even contempt for the rights of the individual citizen by the uniformed representatives of the Republic. Much later we encounter another instance when, despite his general disinclination to write on political subjects, Chou could not help venting his indignation at the events of March 18, 1926, when Tuan Ch'i-jui's soldiers killed twenty-six students who were participating in a political demonstration.[64] In a lengthy article Chou dramatizes the tragedy, without, however, discussing the actual political issues involved.[65]

Under the autocratic rule of the warlords, free political discussion was of course not possible. For the same reason, Chou reports in October, 1926, on a similar incident in Kiukiang only in rather restrained terms.[66] Political criticism often had to be discretely camouflaged, as in the following short essay "Pao-tzu shui" (Tax on Dumplings):

The Ch'ang Mei Hsüan is a Yünnan-Kweichow style eating place in the Central Park [of Peking]; their ham is therefore said to be very good. Not that I have eaten their ham, but I did eat their dumplings with a stuffing made of left-over bits and pieces of ham. They were good and besides also cheap, only two cents per dumpling. Today, finding myself free, I stepped into Central Park and took the opportunity to buy five dumplings at the Ch'ang Mei Hsüan. That would have been ten cents, but, *ayah,* the salesman insisted on another four coppers for what he called something like the "Special Tax on Four Items." Anyone going to a theater, a brothel, a restaurant, or a hotel is to be taxed ten percent, so I would have to pay one cent extra! I told him I had no intention of visiting a theater or brothel; all I wanted was to eat a few dumplings, so why tax me? He said he didn't care, "tax is tax." I just had to pay the four coppers, suffering the loss of four copper-cash. I asked the man whether he knew what the tax was used for. He couldn't say, but thought it might be for the suppression of the "Reds," but he could offer no guarantee. I sat under the cypress trees eating my dumplings and thinking: "How queer, it isn't easy these days to get dumplings; there is no escape from taxation." But then I also thought, if it is really for the suppression of the Reds, we citizens of the capital should be happy to give, because the "Red Horror" is like a "big flood or a fierce animal," and the "White Happiness," how like paradise! We citizens of the capital should know best! [67]

Chou's essays of this period were written at a time when the North China warlords viewed with apprehension the growing strength and increasing ambitions of the Kuomintang party, then in alliance with the Communist party of China and with the Russians. Everything and everyone "Red" or suspected of Red sympathies was therefore suppressed and persecuted without mercy. Chou Tso-jen's greatest concern in this situation, being above all a writer and critic, was naturally the stifling of free expression of opinion, a state of affairs that appeared to him like a return to the Dark Ages of an era thought long past. He wrote:

I feel—I don't know why—that I was born into a dark age. It is true, our woods are free from dragons, tigers, and wolves, but form-less bogies and hobgoblins are still lurking about and biding their chance to swallow the souls of live men. I have little interest in such slogans as "people's ownership," " people's profit," or "freedom of assembly and speech." What I am mostly concerned about is the lack of freedom in a literary prison or in imprisonment for one's creed and beliefs. I was fascinated by the Auto-da-Fé of the Inquisition in the Middle Ages of Western cultural history, the scenes of blazing fires and the black vests of the demons to be burnt.[68]

"Black vests," called "sambenito," were garments condemned sinners were required to wear during and after trial by the Holy Inquisition. Chou Tso-jen continues his sarcastic description of the Spanish Inquisition and concludes with the following state-ment:

What China most urgently needs is to nurture a spirit of tolerance. The present is not a world of culture; it is actually still the time of the Dark Ages of two hundred years ago. The only difference is that formerly you were not allowed to say A, and now you cannot say B. Formerly the emperor ruled, now it is the mob; their tyranny by force is the same. I believe the essence of modern European culture is toler-ance. If we want to cast off barbarism, we have to exert ourselves in this direction. One way is to study the history of struggle in the world of thought. Then we will realize the stupidity and the crime of oppres-sion and how justified it is to oppose [such oppression] and how necessary to achieve tolerance.[69]

National memorial days were of course occasions to compose essays with political overtones. The first such essay from his pen, written in October, 1926, deplores with self-satirizing humor how little there was in the general livelihood of the people or in state affairs to provide reason for rejoicing and celebration. The sarcastic observation is added that the day fell on a Sunday, so that there was not even an extra holiday to be happy about.[70] In 1927, another essay entitled "Shuang-shih-chieh ti kan-hsiang" (Sentiments on the Double Tenth Memorial Day) was to have appeared in the *Yü-ssu* magazine, No. 154, but the whole issue was banned by the police for political reasons.[71] His essay on National Day, 1928, was more optimistic. The five-bar flag, which by its sheer ugliness, Chou had always felt to be a blemish, rather than an adornment, had given way to the Kuomintang flag, the symbol of a new optimism. The only reproach that Chou had at that time was that the National Government had designated the day as Confucius Memorial Day.[72] Old suspicions seem to have been awakened in Chou when he asked: "Is this a sign of a new reaction, this time coming from the South? Is the age of 'much kowtowing and no freedom to speak out' not yet over?" [73] The expression was used, if not coined, by Li Pao-chia in his famous novel *Kuan-ch'ang hsien-hsing chi* (The Present State of Officialdom), a criticism of bureaucracy in the waning years of the Ch'ing dynasty, where this form of sycophantic behavior is given as the secret to success in officialdom.

The above examples demonstrate the manner in which Chou Tso-jen, when dealing with political questions, preferred to point to broader cultural implications rather than engage in shallow polemics. He preferred the humorous, sarcastic manner, witty and provocative suggestiveness to an exhaustive academic discussion of such problems.

VIII *Anti-Confucianism*

Regarding the general social and cultural atmosphere of China in the early years of the Republic, it is a well-known fact that the political break with the past—the abolition of the Manchu regime—had little immediate impact on the ethical, religious, and social thinking of the people. Centuries of indoctrination had firmly embedded neo-Confucianism in the minds of individuals of all classes of society.[74] Only a comparatively small group, mainly foreign-educated intellectuals with little actual power, had been able to free themselves from the mental fetters of traditional thought.

Chou Tso-jen, as has been mentioned above, had studied the Confucian classics in the traditional way at an age when a child cannot possibly be expected to understand, let alone to evaluate critically, the difficult ancient texts, or to realize the various possible interpretations that could be assigned to them. The basic tenets of Confucianism, in a dogmatic late Ch'ing dynasty version, had occupied his attention as a young student. As his critical powers increased, he more and more came to regard Confucianism in this form as nothing but an ideological support for antiquated, unreasonable, and often cruel and harmful institutions, and, in general, as the main obstacle to all social and political progress in China.[75] Liang Ch'i-ch'ao's early writings also strengthened his unequivocal opposition to and rejection of Confucianism. Chou's disbelief in the sacrosanct nature of the old classics was summed up as follows: "I don't believe there is any sacred text in the world that can serve for millennia and centuries as humanity's doctrine." [76]

In its practical application, Confucianism was a harsh code. It governed all human relations, which were formulated in terms of the *san-kang*,[77] the three relations between ruler and subject, husband and wife, father and son; or, expanded to five, the *wu-lun* (five social relations), which included definitions of brotherly love and friendly relations.[78] Apart from relationships between friends, where mutuality on an equal basis was recognized, all other relationships were conceived in terms of strict subordination. The relationship between ruler and subject, or in a wider sense between state and individual if construed in the late-Ch'ing Confucianist sense of an authoritarian relationship, was of course incompatible with the new ideas of democracy and individualism, the tenets of the progressives.[79] In the relationship between father and son, that is, between parents and children, the governing principle according to Confucian doctrine was filial piety, *hsiao,* which by then had come to signify strict subordination within the family hierarchy, with the younger serving the older generation during their lifetime and sacrificing to their spirits when dead.

In this established pattern of social behavior, ancestor worship became one of Chou Tso-jen's first targets of attack. Chou regarded it as an outmoded form of superstitious spiritualism, and as a symbolic act whereby living generations pledge adherence to the ideas, ideals, and institutions bequeathed to them by the dead. In his essay "Ancestor Worship" (1919) he wrote:

We find the custom of ancestor worship in every country of the Far East. Nowadays many uncivilized peoples practice it; in Europe it existed in antiquity. China—strange to say—still practices this backward and uncivilized custom. I think it would only be right to abolish it, since it is contrary to reason and harmful in actual practice.[80]

He goes on to point out the psychological origin of the custom in a primitive spiritualism, namely, in the fear of the living to cause displeasure among the powerful spirits of the departed,[81] and ends: "Now, with the resplendent development of science, we have known for a long time already that there are no ghosts [spirits] and these deceitful sacrificial services [to the ancestors] should of course be abolished." [82] Apart from the material waste involved in the sacrifices, the "holy duty" to have sons—only sons could perform the sacrifices—was often taken as an excuse to indulge in concubinage and related practices.

As to filial piety in particular, this had become another "holy duty," a piece of irrational and unfeeling dogma:

In the house of scholars and higher officials [the traditional Chinese elite, from whom the highest moral standards were expected] the *Twenty-Four Examples of Filial Piety* and the *T'ai-shang kan-ying p'ien* were on the table [as the law of the house], so that even if the father wanted to step down from the position of a tyrannical over-lord to [assume the role of] a close friend [of the other members of the family], it was not possible for him to do so. There have been innumerable cases of this nature. . . . The modern relationship between father and son [on the other hand] takes the relationship between close friends as its supreme model. [83]

Twenty-Four Examples of Filial Piety, first collected in book form by Kuo Chü-yeh of the Yüan dynasty, contains popular stories of extreme feats in service of this virtue. The *T'ai-shang kan-ying p'ien* (Tractate on Actions and Retributions) is generally considered to be the most popular Chinese religious tract. Although Taoist in origin and concept, it mainly contains general ethical admonitions and prohibitions. [84] Chou also pointed out that the Confucian doctrine of *hsiao,* because of its unfeeling emphasis on duty, had not even been able to provide what old people need most, namely, the warm comfort of human affection. Speaking of the needs of old age, Chou said:

They [the aged] will then have to rely on "old friends," and if I do not explicitly refer to "younger family members," but rather jestingly to "old friends," it is not in jest, but because the mention [in this context] of children and grandchildren would seem to emphasize "duty," and the mention of "friends" emphasizes a relationship of affection. In old age it is important to dispel the loneliness that comes with old age. This can only be done by acting in the manner of "old friends," which corresponds to the *yang chih* [care for parents] of antiquity. [85] Still, I don't want to write a sequel to the *Twenty-Four Instances of Filial Piety;* my kind of filial piety, acting in the manner of old friends, is actually very difficult . . . possibly not a

bit easier than the twenty-four instances of filial piety. Why? Because
Chinese family relations, since long ago, have been based on considera-
tions of rank [in the family hierarchy], of benefits and advantages,
rather than on affection.[86]

The extent to which Confucian *hsiao* turned the mind toward
one's ancestry and the past in general was felt by Chou as
being against all logic and basic natural principles. In his essay
"Jen ti wen-hsüeh" (Humane Literature), he states quite bluntly
that the elders exist for their offspring, and not vice versa. He
supports this view with observations from biology and by pointing
to the normal attitude of a healthy society that provides for the
future and does not live for the past:

That parents and grandparents should wear themselves out in the
raising and education of their children, that they do not exact compen-
sation, but just hope to increase wisdom and strength from generation to generation, that is the way of nature. It is also the supreme
way of man. However, in a people of ancester-worshippers, things
are topsy-turvy and therefore in a dilemma.[87]

Another important human relationship, the relationship between husband and wife, had also suffered various degenerative
developments at the hands of the Confucian dogmatists, finally
resulting in the well-known inferior status of women in Chinese
society and the many iniquities ensuing therefrom. In this area,
more than anywhere else, Chou Tso-jen felt that only a basic and
comprehensive reorientation of Chinese thinking could restore
conditions to a natural and healthy state. A new scientific and
psychologically correct way of thinking in matters of sex, discussion of sex problems, and a modern attitude toward the relationship between the sexes was needed. The influence upon Chou's
outlook of the ideas of Havelock Ellis, Edward Carpenter, and
other men of the "New Enlightenment" in England, as has already
been pointed out above, is relevant in this context. Just as these
men had attempted to change European attitudes, Chou tried in
several of his essays relating to the subject of sex relations to
enlighten and reeducate Chinese thinking, to change traditional
social attitudes.

To provide a basis for discussion, the nature and restrictive
limits of traditional morality and concepts of obscenity required
searching examination. Chou's essay "Wei-hsieh lun" (On Ob-

scenity)[88] and his later essay "Wen-i yü tao-te" (Art and Morality)[89] both borrow heavily from Havelock Ellis' thoughts and quote him extensively. In his essay "Wei-hsieh ti ko-yao" (On Obscene Songs),[90] Chou outspokenly defends sex as a permissible topic of, for instance, folk songs, such as were then being collected at Peking University. When a controversy arose over Yü Ta-fu's treatment of sex problems in his novel *Ch'en-lun* (Sinking), Chou wrote a lengthy defense of the work [91] with definitions of immorality based on Mordell's *The Erotic Motive in Literature*.[92] The gist of Chou's argument was that morbid abnormalities, caused by sexual motivations or repressions, may appear in a piece of literature, without making it *ipso facto* immoral and disqualifying it as literature. Only purposely harmful literature, which incites or glorifies evil in man and society, should be disqualified and condemned as immoral. We must not expect of Chou Tso-jen, a believer in Westermarck's ethical relativity, any final answers to the perpetual and universal problem of morality in literature, but there is no doubt that his outspoken treatment of the subject brought about a healthier and more honest attitude toward these questions among his own generation. It was on the achievement of a healthier attitude toward moral values that Chou based his hopes that many related problems, as for instance concubinage, child marriage, forced marriage, female slavery, and the general low status of women in Chinese society, would ultimately find their natural solutions.

However, as time went on, the narrow image of Confucianism as nothing but a reprehensible reactionary social force, as it had appeared to the young, impatient social and ideological reformer, underwent considerable change with growing maturity. Like many another person of his time, Chou came to discover in the Confucian classics, on a restudy of the original texts, much beauty of language and thought, that in his school days had been obscured by perverted interpretations or that had simply remained unrecognized by an immature mind. As he was later to admit:

I don't like to read the books of the Confucian scholars in the *tzu* Section of the *Ssu-k'u*,[93] but the *Lun-yü* (Analects of Confucius) I do read occasionally. Although the language at times is mysterious and some passages obscure and ambiguous, thus remaining beyond my understanding, there are passages that are clear in meaning and furthermore can find our full approval.[94]

And on another occasion:

Some of Confucius' ideas I also like, but unfortunately they were made the ruling ideology and greatly distorted. The more honors were bestowed on Confucianism, the more it lost its true shape. In fact, I am afraid it will be up to us, who know a little of the true meaning, to do some repairs, or rather it seems we should now write our own exegeses of the *Lun-yü.*[95]

We see from these and other passages that Chou's attitude toward Confucianism moved from one of rash, wholesale condemnation to selective appreciation and approval. In this respect, he followed the trend, quite prevalent at the time, of distinguishing between the so-called *li-chiao,* the neo-Confucianism of the later commentators, and the authentic original teachings of the Sage. While neo-Confucianism was viewed as a barrier to social progress and human happiness, it was asserted that the authentic texts, particularly the *Lun-yü,* express many basic human values and much human wisdom that will remain axiomatic truth as long as human society exists. Chou Tso-jen attests to these two aspects of Confucianism when he defines his own position as follows: "I can honestly say of myself that I am a Confucian, but not a Confucianist. I also feel that I am a better friend of Confucius than some of his disciples and offspring." [96]

Since Chou Tso-jen's philosophy of life consisted basically of a belief in scientific truthfulness and humanitarianism, the *humanitas* of the ancient Greeks and of the European Enlightenment, that he should syncretize these beliefs with native Confucianism is no more surprising than the fact that the pioneers of the European Enlightenment, such as Voltaire, Christian Wolff, and Leibniz, all drew inspiration from Confucianism,[97] or at least some basic ideas of it, as were carried back to Europe by the Catholic missionaries.[98] This well-known fact is indeed testimony to the ease of a syncretism between certain Confucian ideas and any set of general humanitarian ideals.

Let us examine for instance Chou Tso-jen's favorite quotation from Confucius: "Knowledge is when you know a thing, to hold that you know it, and when you do not know a thing, to allow that you do not know it" (*Lun yü,* II, 17). This simple saying may merely stand for intellectual honesty, but in its widest possible implications it may stand for the whole Socratic tradition in

European thinking, namely the requirement of logical and scientific analysis and synthesis of all matters. Chou himself pointed this out on several occasions, as, for instance, when he stated: "China's Socrates is Confucius." [99] Or: "I deeply feel this attitude of emphasizing knowledge is the best feature of Chinese thought; it can compare with Socrates; it is the source of the scientific spirit." [100] Chou furthermore signified his great esteem for this principle by deriving from the quoted saying his best known and most frequently used nom de plume, Chih-t'ang (Knowledge/Wisdom Studio), as he explains himself:

Confucius said: "Knowledge/wisdom is when you know a thing, to hold that you know it, and when you do not know a thing, to allow that you do not know it." Hsün-tzu said: "To say the appropriate thing, that is wisdom; to be silent at the appropriate time, that too is wisdom." [101] These are excellent words and I shall use them to name my own *t'ang* (studio). Of old there was Yang Hsi-fu,[102] who would not accept bribes and who held forth on the four wisdoms. Posterity admired his lofty integrity and used this [reference to four wisdoms] to formulate a *t'ang* name for him [namely, Ssu-chih-t'ang, or "Four Wisdom Studio"]; this was indeed long ago. My *t'ang* name, being chosen later, should perhaps be *Hsin* Ssu-chih-t'ang (*New* Four Wisdoms Studio). However Confucius and Hsün-tzu [from whom Chou derived his studio name] lived at the time of the [ancient] Chou dynasty; they are certainly not "new." Furthermore wisdom/knowledge should not be limited to four kinds. I therefore cut away half [of Hsin Ssu-chih-t'ang] and took only Chih-t'ang (Knowledge/Wisdom Studio) as my *t'ang* name.[103]

The other great ideal of Chou Tso-jen's philosophy of life, humanitarianism, is indeed easy to retrace in Confucianism to the concept of *jen*.[104] Chou himself once expressed the following opinion on *jen*: "The central idea of Confucianism is *jen*. If subdivided, it becomes *chung* (loyalty) and *shu* (reciprocity), and, taken as a whole, if you don't like "humanitarianism" because it may lead to misinterpretation, "you may call it 'the path of man.' " [105] The Confucian classics contain many pronouncements on *jen*.[106] The first seven sayings in Book Four of the *Lun-yü* speak of *jen*. Another classic, the *Chung-yung* (Chapter Twenty, paragraph five), contains the short sentence "jen-che jen-yeh ("humanitas" is man), which Mencius repeats, (*Meng-tzu*, Chapter "chin-hsin, hsia," paragraph sixteen), and which Legge translates as

"Benevolence [*jen*] is the distinguishing characteristic of man." All these definitions confirm the identity of *jen* and "humanitas" or "humanitarianism." [107] In the same way that Confucianism views *jen* as the root from which the stem and branches of the human personality and human society should grow forth, it is also Chou's conviction that perfection of the individual into a truly humane being is rudimentary and prerequisite to the solution of social problems and the creation of a better society. [108] Not only as regards *chih* and *jen,* but also as regards both the general method of approaching problems and personal bearing and conduct, do we find that Chou followed Confucian tradition in propounding an attitude of *chung-yung.* The difficulty of expressing *chung-yung* in a modern language caused him to translate it with the ancient Greek word *sophrosyne,* thereby demonstrating the similarity of certain aspects in Confucianism with those of the European humanist tradition.

Although Chou Tso-jen never relinquished his hostility toward neo-Confucianism for what it had done to impede social progress, he did very frankly and somewhat proudly admit in 1944 that the Confucian tradition had been strongly implanted in him:

I myself admit that I belong to the *ju-chia* [scholars, usually meaning "Confucian scholars"] school of thought, but this designation of *ju-chia* is all mine, and I am afraid my interpretation of it may differ greatly from the general opinion. I think Chinese thinking emphasizes being a "man proper," the *ju-chia's* propounding of *jen* [humanitas] and *chung-yung* [temperance] is just to the same effect. It may be in order for me to apply the designation of *ju-chia* to myself, but this is because Confucius was a Chinese; that is why it is like this. It is not because Confucius established a religion and preached the Way that Chinese became followers of the *ju* teaching. [109]

There is a certain "supra-denominational" connotation in the above. The implication is that Confucius was only a spokesman for, but did not substantially add to nor change, Chinese cultural values that originated and were already firmly shaped long before his time, and that thenceforth ran uninterruptedly through all subsequent Chinese thought and intellectual activity. This development is one to which H. G. Creel has applied the term "Sinism." [110] This interpretation of Confucian values was important to Chou Tso-jen, because, on the one hand, he wanted to disassociate himself from a Confucianism that lent itself to narrow dogmatic interpretations, and, on the other hand, he consciously felt that the Chinese tradition, of which Confucianism in its broader implications was so much a part, was a vital source of his own strength and productivity.[111]

By acknowledging a kind of "Sinism" as a common denominator of all Chinese philosophy and religion, Chou achieved a sensible compromise and at the same time also acknowledged the osmotic influences of the "three Chinese religions" on each other during the centuries that they had existed side by side. Their borderlines had become blurred, and the patterns of their organizations, their rituals, and even parts of their dogmas had become similar.[112] If Chou still occupied himself above all with Confucianism, this was probably due to the fact that Confucianism was the most prominent force within the strata of society to which he belonged, that he could observe best, and that he wrote about with great knowledge and authority.

IX *Attitudes Toward Buddhism and Taoism*

Apart from Confucianism, however, Buddhism and Taoism were active forces in the Chinese social context that Chou Tso-jen could not altogether disregard. In fact, in his younger years, he had once made a determined study of Buddhism. As he described it in a biographical essay:

The most common department within the "miscellany of my studies" one can probably say is the study of Buddhist scriptures. But, as in the case in Chinese literature, I am here not orthodox, so that my way is different from that of other students of the Buddhist texts. Forty years ago in Nanking I was once a humble disciple of a Buddhist layman by the name of Yang Jen-shan.[113] I was favored with instructions in the way to attain Nirvana, but, although I studied various translations of Amitabha sutras and found descriptions of the "Happy Land of Tranquil Nourishment" most interesting, and although I also had some understanding of the idea that one had first to attain Nirvana and then practice pious conduct (somewhat like first trying to enter and live in a foreign settlement and then making a good go of it), I had no interest in carrying out [the instructions given me]. I was interested in the *Recorded Admonitions* of the Meditation School of Buddhism, but actually failed to fully understand them. As for *ch'an* (meditation) and *cheng* (attainment of ultimate truth), just as in the story of the monk who asked the depth of a rivulet and was pushed into it from a bridge, I can understand the meaning and admire it,

but I for one have no intention to "jump into it." That I read the
Recorded Admonitions without great ambitions is regrettable; the few
books that I bought on this subject are therefore resting on the shelves.
The lofty and deep dogma of Buddhism seem to belong to the sphere
of psychology and mysticism. I studied them, but am not certain at
all that I understand them. I therefore did not dare make deeper
enquiries into the Fa-hsiang school of Buddhism [114] or such matters.
Summing up: if one does not follow one of these broad roads, one
cannot penetrate Buddhism. I merely read the Buddhist texts as
literature; they represent specimens of classical Chinese and what I
got out of reading them was therefore naturally only [an appreciation
of their substance as] prose literature and [philosophical] thought, and
nothing else. [115]

Considered as literature, the Buddhist scriptures impressed Chou
as excellent achievements of the art of translation; he regarded
them as "a glorious chapter in the history of translation." [116]
In view of his own experiences in translating foreign works, his
admiration is certainly the judgment of an expert in the field.
Uninterested in Buddhist dogma, he was nevertheless attracted in
his diligent, even though somewhat amateurish way, to the ethno-
logical and anthropological aspects of Buddhist mythology. The
custom of distributing beans and bean-cake on Buddha's birthday, for instance, in order to "contract an affinity," and the
Buddhist concepts of *yüan* and *yeh* made him speculate whether
these ideas were not the ancient roots of our "modern" concepts
of heredity and environment, although couched in the more
poetical language of the past. [117] Believing that many Buddhist
beliefs and practices of the time had degenerated into superstitious ritual, [118] he publicly condemned them as such. [119] Popular
Taoism, which to an even greater extent had become a vehicle
for various and sundry popular superstitions, was similarly
regarded as a degenerate set of beliefs and practices.

Taoism, in Chou's opinion, was the largest beneficiary among
the three religions of whatever religious needs or sentiments existed
among the people, particularly among the peasant masses of rural
China. There was nothing left in popular Taoism of the original
natural cosmology of Lao-tzu; instead, Taoism had degenerated
into a cult of magical practices. [120] Owing to its great popularity,
it had been able to attain a position of almost unassailable power
over the minds of the people in the countryside. It no longer

possessed any coherent, discernible dogma of its own; therefore, it tended to accommodate whatever local superstitions it encountered and to adapt from Confucianism and Buddhism whatever appealed to the primitive mind of the ignorant, to whom it mostly catered. A belief in the transmigration of souls and the concepts of monastic organization were both borrowed from Buddhism. Elements of ancestor worship that had their origin in the Confucian idea of filial piety were also adapted to Taoist needs. An example is the following story recounted by Chou:

In an article entitled "Pity the Old Man" in the *Hsin-sheng-huo* (New Life) Magazine, [the story is told of] an old man who raised and supported a good-for-nothing son by the sweat of his brow. His reason: "If I chase my son out, who will burn paper money for me when I am dead!" . . .Confucius once said: "Sacrifice [to the ancestors with devotion and attentively] as if they were present," [121] but later Confucianist practitioners mostly went over to the Taoist concept of worshipping the soul merely out of fear that the roaming spirit [of a deceased person] might suffer hunger [and vent its displeasure on the living].[122]

This sense of constant threat from spirits and demons, and the duty imposed on the living of ritual sacrifices and burnt offerings, is one of the many evils of Taoism that Chou castigates in his essay "Hsiang-ts'un yü tao-chiao ssu-hsiang" (The Village and Taoist Thought). Another belief which he deplored was predetermination, the idea that fate assigns each person a fixed station in life. This idea, he believed, stifled ambition and desire for improvement and reform.

Taoism also invented its own hierarchy of deities, of whom the higher bore titles of "emperor," a fact which, in Chou's opinion, kept the population "emperor-minded" decades after the establishment of the Republic. In the same essay, he first sardonically suggests that Catholic Christianity could perhaps provide a solution by converting the many little Taoist deities into saints of the Church! In a more serious vein, he argued that the only solution to the problem was the education of the masses. The second part of this essay was written six years later, and he observed, "Everything changes fast, the *Hsin-sheng-huo* magazine, in which the first part appeared, ceased publication long ago. Only one thing has remained, namely, the Taoist way of thinking of the people!"

Native Chinese medicine, which flourished under the aegis of Taoism, was attacked in the same essay:

There is no sense in the terms "Chinese medicine" and "Western medicine," and we should rather speak of a struggle between old and new medicine.[123] I never could understand the talk of "Chinese studies for substance, foreign studies for techniques," [124] or [the slogan] "Eastern culture is superior to Western culture." In my opinion, there is only one culture because there is only one humanity; there are merely differences in tastes brought about by variety in basically uniform cultures. In the end all point in the same direction that humanity will take in its progress. . . . I also believe there is only one science, one art, but due to earlier or later development they have assumed varying forms. Levels of development differ, but not their substance. Chinese medicine does not belong only to China; Western medicine is not solely owned by Westerners. There is fundamentally only one medical science, and both, Chinese and Western medicine, are merely stages of development of the whole science of medicine. In order of time, it may be permissible to speak of "earlier" and "later," "old" and "new," but it is not permissible to differentiate by location into "Eastern" and "Western," "Chinese" and "foreign." [125]

The bold formulation of the principle of the universality of science and the cosmopolitan spirit which this reflects are certainly commendable.[126] If some of his condemnations now appear too sweeping in view of later scientific confirmation of the efficacy of some native healing methods and drugs,[127] his criticism was generally justified for its castigation of the stubborn refusal of traditionalists to benefit from modern scientific methods. To prove how closely this type of native medicine was linked with culturally reactionary elements, Chou cited the interesting fact that Chang Chih-chao's calligraphy adorned the decorative name-board over the door of the College of Chinese Native Medicine and Pharmaceutics in Peking, the door that Chou had to pass almost daily on his way to work.[128] Chang Shih-chao had started out as a revolutionary when he was connected with the *Su-pao* newspaper in Shanghai in 1903, but later changed to the reactionary camp. He was the leading spirit behind the *Chia-yin* magazine that opposed the new culture movement. In the Tuan Ch'i-jui regime, he served as minister of education and instigated the repressive actions which resulted, for instance, in the removal of Lu Hsün from Peking Normal College, following student demonstrations there. In more recent times, Chang performed a successful changeover to communism.[129]

X *Attitude Toward Christianity*

Chou's attitude toward the three Chinese religions, as we have seen, had been one of outright hostility, except perhaps with regard to certain ancient Chinese social and ethical traditions that had been incorporated into Confucianism and that Chou was willing to recognize as of universal validity and value. The foreign religion, Christianity, that had reappeared in China in the nineteenth century with new vigor and in the company of many other enticing new ideas, presented another challenge that Chou felt drawn to explore in his essays.

That Chou once intended to retranslate the Bible from the Greek into Chinese has been mentioned before. This fact alone indicates his interest in and due recognition of the importance of Christianity in the cultural development of Europe. However, his interest in the Bible was not religiously motivated. As a man whose faith was a syncretism of Confucianism and the Greek ideal of *humanitas,* his whole personality and mentality was averse to the mystic and the metaphysical in any system of religious belief. Belief in Christianity, too, would have been incongruous in a man of Chou's dispositions and way of thinking. His approach to Christianity was from the start and throughout his life exclusively rational; it was an exercise in eclectic syncretizing. Chou admired and recognized the greatness of Christ and his teachings as illustrious examples of an ultra-humanitarianism.[130] "If I were strong enough, I would shoulder the cross and follow Christ," he once exclaimed.[131] In moments of calmer reflection he rejected all dogma—and we may infer that he also included here Christian dogma—that asked of man the performance of "ultra-human" deeds.[132] He defines this term as sacrifice merely for the sake of pure altruism, sacrifice for which reason cannot provide convincing justification in terms of personal benefit.

If Christianity did not possess an ultimate persuasiveness for Chou, it at least provided occasion to demonstrate his own humanitarian temperance and religious tolerance, when, in 1922, a "Students' Anti-Religious Movement"[133] tried to stir up anti-Christian sentiment in the populace. Chou "remained apart from the prevalent bombast and hysteria," according to one observer;[134] in fact, together with four other professors of National Peking University, he published a statement asserting the right of the individual to choose his own religion.[135] There is a personal testimony to affirm that although Chou himself did not feel a need for Christianity, he would not deny freedom of religion to anyone, but required only that religious organizations not impede freedom of thought or scientific inquiry.[136]

XI Cultivation of European Literary Interests

On analyzing Chou's attitudes toward religion, we have been able to show his views concerning an extremely wide area of intellectual endeavor and social relations, because religion, in a very broad sense of the word, was so powerful and all-pervading a reactionary social force in China that it presented the most natural and most conspicuous target for reformers like Chou Tso-jen. However, beyond the struggle for social reform and the particular questions relevant to that movement, a very considerable segment of his essays was concerned with larger cultural interests. He worked continuously to broaden his knowledge and understanding of the literature of Europe and Japan. Simultaneously, he attempted to introduce to the Chinese reading public whatever appealed to him most by translating from these literatures or by writing of them in his essays.

As regards European literature, it is interesting to note that studies of anthropological, folkloric, and mythological themes occupied his attention during the 1920's and 1930's. The essays he wrote at that time make frequent mention of J. G. Frazer's *The Golden Bough.* He also acknowledges his indebtedness to Frazer's "Scope of Social Anthropology," an addendum to the second edition of *Psyche's Task,*[137] and to the studies of Andrew Lang.[138] Greek antiquity and mythology was also a never ending subject of personal interest. Particular mention is made of the studies of W. H. D. Rouse and Jane E. Harrison. The *Yung-jih-chi* contains a translation of the third chapter of Harrison's *Greek Mythology* (1924) under the heading "Lun Shan-mu," [139] while his contributions to the *Yü-ssu* magazine contain a large proportion of translations from Greek mythology.[140] When P'u-i, the last emperor of China, was ejected from his domain in the Forbidden City of Peking, Chou addressed an open letter to the youthful former emperor and seriously suggested that he could give his life new and meaningful purpose by taking up the study of Greek antiquity.[141]

From his earlier student days in Japan, Chou also carried over into his later years an abiding interest—indeed, an almost religious belief, in Havelock Ellis. In his essay "Ai-li-ssu ti hua" (Words on Ellis), written in 1924, he elaborates on Ellis' idea that moral restraints must not be imposed by outside coercion, like church asceticism, but rather must be understood as nature's give and take, that is as an inherent, sane natural law, and must be accepted in this sense and to that extent. Perhaps we see here another attempt to bring together the ideas of Ellis and the Confucian concept of *chung-yung*. *Chou* also admired the picture that Ellis painted of the ideal man as a torchbearer in a relay race. In the space of his allotted time he will carry the torch forward, advance enlightenment in his generation, and at the end he will be ready to hand the torch to the next runner in this continuous progression of human knowledge and culture, while himself dropping back again into the darkness of oblivion.[142] In 1925, Chou published translations of Ellis's *Impressions and Comments* (1913–23), and later in 1928, Chou also acknowledged the "careful study" of Ellis' work of social philosophy, the *New Spirit* (1926).[143]

Purely literary interests in European writers motivated Chou to translate numerous works into Chinese. Apart from his early cooperative venture with his brother Lu Hsün, the *Yü-wai hsiao-shuo chi* (Collection of Foreign Short Stories), he published most of his translations of the 1920's and 1930's in the *Hsin-ch'ing-nien* (New Youth), the *Hsiao-shuo yüeh-pao* (Short Story Monthly), *Wen-hsüeh chou-pao* (Literary Weekly), and the *Yü-ssu* (Threads of Talk). Jonathan Swift is represented by two pieces, the "Directions to Servants" and "A Modest Proposal." [144] It was Swift's humor and satire that he later held up as ideals of humorous writing. Strindberg is represented by two stories from his early collection *Married* (1884), both humorous, with social criticism and the conflict between the sexes as underlying themes.[145] His interest in the weak and oppressed peoples of Eastern Europe, where he also chose for translation lesser known writers, such as Sologub, Kuprin, Andreev, and the Polish author Zeromski, remained proportionately strong, however. In 1920, Chou brought out an anthology of such translations in *Tien-ti* (Drops), which was republished with minor changes as *K'ung-ta-ku* (Empty Drums) in 1928. This book reappeared in a third edition as late as 1939, testifying to the public appeal of the short, unassuming stories which made up the collection, and to the translator's skill. Other favorites that Chou chose for translation were the Hungarian writer Mor Jokai, the Greek writer Ephtaliotis, and Hans Christian Andersen.[146]

As a result of the courses he taught in European literature at Peking University, Chou compiled a textbook on the history of European literature, *Ou-chou wen-hsüeh shih,* which for its time (1918) was a pioneering work, though perhaps not of great literary or pedagogic merit.[147] Several other literary treatises of this time on such topics as "Russia and China in Literature," "Views on Women in European Ancient Literature," "The Poems of William Blake," and so forth, are somewhat dry and long-winded.[148] They are indeed academic treatises rather than casual essays and are mainly interesting in this context as revealing Chou's intellectual interests at that time.

XII *Cultivation of Japanese Literary Interests*

In the field of Japanese literature, Chou Tso-jen's arduous efforts to transmit some of his knowledge of Japanese cultural life to the Chinese reading public were performed under the dual disadvantages of a steadily growing militarism in Japan and an aggressive Japanese policy toward China, a policy that had begun to take ominous form after World War I and that accelerated in the postwar years. The Japan that Chou had known as a young student had changed; the Japan he knew was the Japan of culture and humanitarianism, of the Heian cultural tradition, and of the Shirakaba writers,[149] a world to which he had become extremely attached. In the gradually deteriorating situation of the 1920's and 1930's, he felt that all he could do was to use his knowledge of a better Japan and try to communicate to his less knowledgeable fellow countrymen some sense of Japanese cultural attainments, just as he also attempted to make known China's position to his Japanese friends.[150] All this was done in the hope that he might contribute to the improvement of mutual understanding and respect between the two peoples that were both dear to his heart.

How little he succeeded is sad to contemplate, but the situation at least did not seem to have discouraged him from pursuing most diligently his studies of Japan's cultural past and of her contemporary writers, for whom he held great admiration. He felt it was his duty to point out to his Chinese readers the shallowness of their knowledge of Japan and their resulting incorrect judgment of the Japanese people as a whole. The expression "Ch'in Jih p'ai" (Friends of Japan) had become a common term of abuse in the politically poisoned atmosphere of the time. Chou nevertheless used this very epithet as the title of an essay,[151] wherein he asserts that, objectively speaking, the term cannot really apply to any Chinese, because China has so far never produced a true friend of Japan, for the reason that no Chinese had ever penetrated deeply enough into Japanese culture, as had, for instance, Lafcadio Hearn, the Anglo-American, who could indeed qualify as a "friend of Japan." This shallow knowledge of Japan, Chou considered a serious shortcoming; he therefore advised his fellow Chinese to study the cultures of other peoples instead of brandishing about meaningless slogans.

In another essay, Chou objected strongly to the widespread notion that Japanese culture was noncreative and imitative as a frivolous and superficial attitude based on false premises, since cultural borrowing, he argued, is universal and commendable.[152] He reminded his Chinese readers of the fact that, whatever the influences of the *Shih-ching* may have been, the *Manyōshū* and the *Kojiki* stand out as evidence of Japanese creativity in the literary realm.[153] "The first chapter of the *Kojiki* contains myths comparable in beauty only to those of Greece, and certainly nowhere found in the alleged prototype of Ssu-ma Ch'ien." In the same connection, Chou also referred to the novels of the Heian period, for instance the *Genji Monogatari*,[154] that in type and literary excellence predate Chinese novels of equal quality by about five hundred years. Only during the Edo period (1603–1867) did the popular literature of China attain approximately the same level as that reached in Japan. In more recent times, beginning shortly after the Meiji Restoratiton, literary achievements in Japan again surpassed those in China, being roughly thirty years ahead of similar developments in China. Meiji literature seemed to forecast exactly the path that China's New Literature Movement was to take and is still in the process of following.

The object of this comparison was to show how much China had still to learn from Japan, even in the field of literary endeavor in which the Chinese had become accustomed to feel unquestionably superior. During the years that Chou was writing, the cultural scene in Japan was beginning to pale under the shadow of a growing reactionary trend in politics. A particularly blatant case of interference with freedom of thought and expression was the imprisonment of Professor Inoue Tetsujiro (1856–1944) for lese majesty. Professor Inoue's scholarly investigations had cast doubt upon the antiquity of one of the Three Sacred Articles of the Shinto cult. This case induced Chou to write a scathing satirical essay on "The Literary Prison of a Civilized Country." [155] A similar case was also discussed by him in the essay "Kuan-yü jen-shen mai-mai" (On Slave Trade).[156] It concerned Sano Manabu's *Social History of Japan* (1922), which was banned by the Japanese authorities because of its criticism of contemporary social conditions.

Japanese militarism, even in the early 1920's, was the great obstacle to mutual understanding and respect between the two peoples, and Chou did not hesitate frankly to say so: "We know that the Japanese [who exploit the weakness of the Chinese people] are a group of militarists. We must oppose them, in the same way that we must oppose rapacious elements in our own country." [157] Chou also focused attention upon the evil influences attending the arrival in China of hordes of Japanese "carpet-baggers" who followed in the wake of expanding Japanese military power.[158] He also expressed criticism of Japanese pseudo-intellectuals, namely, the so-called *Chih-na-t'ung* (China Expert).[159] This Japanese version of the "Old China Hand" particularly outraged Chou because the *Chih-na-t'ung* claimed and was credited with expert knowledge of China and the Chinese, while he actually engaged in malicious slander, reporting exclusively and often in an exaggerated manner on objectionable, seamy aspects of Chinese life. The expression *Chih-na-t'ung* occurs in several of his essays of the 1930's. In "Chih-na min-tsu-hsing" (The Chinese National Character),[160] he criticizes a product typical of a *Chih-na-t'ung*, namely, the book *The National Character of the Chinese as Gleaned from Their Novels,* by Yasuoka Hideo.[161] In summing up, Chou states:

We do not expect Japan to flatter us or to defend China; we only hope that she will express her exhortations and reproof sincerely and in a dignified manner. However, the flippant and frivolous attitudes of the *Chih-na-tung* should be avoided under all circumstances. Because I love Japanese culture I do not want this flippancy to become a trait of the national character of the Japanese people.[162]

The theme reappears even as late as 1943. During the war many Chinese students were sent from the Japanese-occupied districts of the mainland to study in Japan, and, incidentally, to be persuaded of Japan's role in all of East Asia. However, many returned from periods of study in Japan with deep resentment, rather than admiration, for the Japanese people. To explain this somewhat embarrassing phenomenon, Chou courageously points to the *Chih-na-t'ung* and the defamatory anti-Chinese reporting as the main cause of such reactions among these students.[162]

In a more positive sense, Chou did much to introduce Japanese cultural values to his fellow countrymen, mostly through numerous translations from the Japanese. Throughout his long career, Chou never ceased to translate representative works of Japanese literature. His early admiration, dating from his years as a student in Japan,[163] was for the modern realists and humanitarian writers, usually identified as the Shirakaba group, whose strong influence on his own mentality and work he was always ready to admit.[164] The most famous names of this group, like Mushakoji Saneatsu, Kunikida Doppo,[165] Natsume Sōseki,[166] Mori Ōgai,[167] Arishima Takeo,[168] are represented in Chou's anthology of translations from the Japanese, the *Hsien-tai Jih-pen hsiao-shuo chi* (A Collection of Modern Japanese Short-Stories). This collection contains thirty translations from fifteen writers; eleven of the translations are by his older brother Lu Hsün. All the writers represented in the collection belonged to the modern, realist school, which propagated humanitarian values and criticized contemporary social conditions, without, however, thereby impairing the belletristic character and quality of their finely rendered short stories.[169] No doubt this collection was also meant to serve as a model, in both form and content, for contemporary Chinese writers.

Particular mention should be made of Chou's translations of the works of Yosano Akiko.[170] In her essays on questions of sex, morals, and the status of women, she expressed ideas that Chou himself had long approved of. By translating her essays into Chinese, Chou showed again his strong interest in these topics, which, after all, occupied an important area within what may be called the modernization of Chinese thought in general.[171]

Chou also singled out other Japanese literary figures, devoting essays to their life stories and works. The novelist Bakin,[172] the *haibun* writer Issa,[173] the poet Ishikawa Takuboku,[174] and the writers Shimazaki Tōson,[175] Arishima Takeo, and Mori Ōgai received special consideration in this manner. In the case of Bakin and Issa, Chou seems to have been attracted by unconventional elements in their personalities and their lives, which were also reflected in their literary works. This is particularly the case with Issa, the Buddhist monk who roamed the countryside all alone and lived in disregard of narrow monastic rules or dogmas, and who also inspired Mushakoji to write a short play about him, a play which Chou later translated into Chinese. Chou Tso-jen's characterization of Issa's writings is given in his essay "Jih-pen shih-jen I-ch'a ti shih" (The Poetry of the Japanese Poet Issa), where he says:

The Japanese *haiku* as such defies translation; Issa's *haiku* poems are even more "untranslatable." The *haiku* is a short, seventeen syllable poem that mainly describes its object indirectly by hint and suggestion. It therefore sounds simple, clear, and suggestive, but its full meaning lies beyond the literal level. If translated in a direct manner, its main characteristics are unavoidably lost. Issa's phrases are peculiar; because of his peculiar circumstances, he developed an eccentric and also compassionate nature. His poems cast off the abstract and contemplative flavor of unperturbed solitude, as found in Matsuo Bashō, and return to the almost jocular and playful style of Matsunaga Teitoku. However, there is a basic difference because his jesting contains human sympathy, and his cold laughter is filled with hot tears. His opposition to the mighty and his sympathy for the weak all grow from one root. He does not have the unperturbed solitude of the Bashō school, but in the jesting of the Teitoku school there is none of his warmth of sympathy. Among the Japanese *haiku* poets, Issa was and is quite unique; some therefore call him a comet in the *haiku* cosmos; he suddenly appeared, and likewise he disappeared all of a sudden, without leaving a trace behind [i.e., none continued his type of artistry].

Chou also compiled the first comprehensive survey in Chinese of the development of the modern Japanese short story in his "Jih-pen chin san-shih nien hsiao-shuo chih fa-ta" (Development of the Japanese Novel in the Last Thirty Years), which had originally been the subject of a lecture at Peking University, but later appeared as an article in the Hsin-ch'ing-nien (New Youth) magazine.[176] In this article, Chou defends cultural borrowing and appeals to Chinese writers to follow the Japanese example in developing a prose literature of modern form and content. The didactic purpose to show his countrymen how to write good short stories should not, however, be taken as his major motivation in undertaking this work. Mainly, his translations from Japanese literature were motivated by a genuine desire to transmit purely artistic and cultural values. In his early years, for instance, Chou had already translated a number of *kyōgen* plays, attracted by their down-to-earth and folksy realism and their display of old folk tales and folk beliefs.[177] Guided by the same bent for the popular, near-to-life element, a bent that we can observe throughout his life, Chou translated the more popular components of the ancient *Kojiki* anthology under the heading "Ku-shih-chi chung ti lien-ai ku-shih" (Love Stories from the Kojiki). Other stories from the *Kojiki* followed later.[178]

In Japanese poetry, *haiku* poetry particularly fascinated him for its special transcendental quality. The *haiku* is unique in world poetry for its economy of expression.[179] It does no more than suggest a mood or thought; it is then left to the reader to go beyond the literal level of the poem. This so-called lingering effect on the mind of the reader was also an effect much sought after by essay writers—as it was by Chou Tso-jen himself—because the essay is also a literary form of limited extent that usually requires supplementation by the reader's own emotional and mental processes, as they are invoked and stimulated by the reading of the essay.

Significantly, Chou was also much interested in the *haiku's* more popular derivative, the *kyoku,* also called *senryu,*[180] which is of a humorous, satirical, and sometimes even vulgar character. In his opinion, it was nonetheless admirable for its direct expression of genuine popular sentiment. As he expressed it:

The good *senryu* shows its excellence in grasping realistically the main points of a situation and in projecting them without polite restraints and with a deeper meaning. The reader is made to feel a prick, as of a needle. It is like eating mustard, which may be sharp and bring tears to the eyes, but the sharpness will pass quickly and will not stick to the tongue, like when eating green peppers.[181]

XIII *Contemplations and Descriptions*

As previously stated with reference to the modern Japanese short story, and which bears repeating in a more general form, the utilitarian and didactic aspects of Chou's essays, while fairly strong in a number of his essays, should neither be taken as main motivations, nor as constituting their main values. The literary excellence of his essays derives mainly from an excellence of form and mood, from the general style of writing. In discussing the content of his essays, it behooves us to emphasize again that it was in the field of the contemplative, nontendentious, nondogmatic essay that Chou Tso-jen achieved the high level of perfection for which he is justly renowned.

Typical essays of this kind frequently do not bear eye-catching titles. Instead, they appeared in unobtrusive sections of literary magazines under such headings as "Random Notes," "Leisure Talk," "Sundry Sentiments," "Correspondence," and the like, and are characteristically ephemeral notes on minor affairs and personal impressions of the moment. Yet, they possess an artistic quality all their own, are simple yet meaningful observations on small incidents from life, such as the enjoyment of what nature and life offer, or the art of making life beautiful and enjoyable. Not the least of their merits is the well-adjusted, relaxed, good-humored, and optimistic frame of mind which informs them.

By way of illustration, the translation of a letter Chou wrote to a friend who had enquired about his native place, Shaohsing, can be cited. Chou replied:

From your letter I see that you are going to visit my native place. You want me to give you some guidance. Frankly speaking, my great love is not exactly for that place, but since I grew up there and lived there for over ten years, I do indeed know a little of its conditions, and therefore write to let you know.

I don't want to tell you about the countryside and the people. If I were to do that, I would never finish writing. However, once you get there, you will clearly see all that for yourself, and there is no need for me to bother you with redundant comments. I want to limit myself here to one most interesting item, namely, boats. In your native place you usually ride in a ricksha, streetcar, or motorcar, but these don't exist in my native place. Apart from sedan-chairs used inside the city or in the mountains, the ordinary means of conveyance are boats. There are two kinds of boats, those ordinarily used are the *wu-p'eng* (black awning) boats. The *pai-p'eng* (white awning) boats are mostly used for longer trips. To go on one of these on a night trip to Hsi-ling has also its special attraction, but since you will hardly be riding on one of them, I am not going to discuss them here.

Among the *wu-p'eng* boats, the larger ones are called *ssu-ming-wa* (four transparent tiles), and the smaller are called *chiao-hua* (foot punted) boats, or just "small boats," but the most suitable ones are the in-betweens, called *san-tao* (three sections), or *san-ming-wa* (three transparent tiles). The awning is semi-circular, woven from bamboo strips with a bamboo stick down the middle, and daubed with black oil. Between two sections of fixed awnings there is a sun-shade, also semi-circular, consisting of a wooden frame inlaid with large fish-scales of about one inch each. It is quite transparent, like glass, but also very strong in use. That is what is called *ming-wa* (transparent tile). The so-called *san-ming-wa* is a boat that has two shades in the middle and one in the back of the boat. At the stern there are usually two sculls and in the front there is a bamboo punting pole to direct the boat. At the stem it has eyes and eyebrows, as of a tiger, but seemingly with an enigmatic smile, quite funny and not fearful. There is none of this on the white awning boats. In the *san-tao* boats the awning is probably high enough to permit you to stand, and the compartment is wide enough for a square table so that four persons can sit and play Mahjong—I suppose you have learnt that already?

The "small boats" are really like "leaves floating on the waves." [182] When you sit on the mat at the bottom of the boat, the awning is only two or three inches from your head. You can put both hands on the sides of the boat; in that kind of boat, you feel like you are sitting on the water. Passing the rice fields, the banks almost touch your face. Then, if there should be wind or waves, or if you are just a little careless and don't sit steady, the boat may capsize and you might be in danger, but that too might be good fun, a specialty of the "water country." However, in your case, you had better use one of the *san-tao* boats.

When you go on a boat trip though, don't be hurried as when riding a streetcar, expecting to reach your destination almost immediately. If you leave the city for a trip of about thirty or forty miles (our mile there is very short, about one third of an English mile), you should count on one day for the return trip. When going by one of these boats, do so in a mood of going sightseeing into the country. Watch everything around you, the mountains that will be visible everywhere, the tallow trees on the shore, the smartweed on the river banks, the fishermen's huts, and all shapes and kinds of bridges. When you are tired, take a nap inside the compartment, take some essays along to read, or pour yourself a cup of tea. Outside P'ien-men gate, the Chien-hu area, the Ho-chia lake, or in the vicinity of Hu-shang, all these places I like very much. You could perhaps also go to Lou-kung-fu and visit the Lan-t'ing [183] by donkey (but I rather advise you to walk, the donkey ride may not be the right thing for you). When the sky darkens in sunset colors and you enter the East Gate with the *hsieh-chih* [184] draped over the walls, it is a most interesting sight.

If the roads are not safe, you should start your trip to Hangchow by boat in the afternoon. The landscape at dusk is really beautiful. Unfortunately, I have forgotten the place-names in that area. At night when you rest in the compartment and hear the noise of the water and the oars, the greetings shouted between passing boats, the barking of dogs and crowing of cocks in the villages, that is really quite an experience!

When you rent a boat and attend the temple fair, you can get a true idea of the old Chinese stage plays. On the boat you are completely at ease to do as you like. If you want to, you watch the show, or you may sleep, if you prefer, or have some wine. In my opinion it is the ideal way of enjoying oneself. It is only too bad that with all the talk of "reforms," these stage shows and fairs have been prohibited. Some middle-class boors have now set up a theater of "ocean-wide" dimensions in the Piecegoods Merchants Guild House and are inviting everybody to buy tickets and see the "cattish" shows from Shanghai. On no account go to such places! I am afraid you will be a complete stranger when you get to my native place, but because I am teaching, I cannot join you in the fun of riding the night boat or having a leisurely chat. I apologize and also regret it very much. . . .[185]

We find in this letter-essay several of the elements typical of Chou's contemplative essays. The essay is not altogether without its purpose; the letter was after all written to convey information. The information is detailed, even almost pedantic on certain points. It concerns the author's favorite subject of folkways; it is in part an anthropological study of the boats used in the Shaohsing area. But, in most senses, it is not an exhaustive treatise. Usually, it merely hints at lines of thought capable of further development, as, for instance, in the case of rural stage plays as a means of studying the primitive origins of the drama, a subject on which Chou himself has elaborated on other occasions.[186] Throughout the essay breathes the personality of the writer, his evaluation of what is and what is not enjoyable. Above all, it reflects his insouciant philosophy of life, that one can find ideal enjoyment in an untrammeled and unhurried boat ride, with the peaceful, soothing, and faint noises of the water and countryside in the background.

Other essays of a similar nature are found, for instance, in the series "Ts'ao mu ch'ung yü" (Plants, Trees, Insects, Fish), in which scarecrows, pickled vegetables, bats, goldfish, and lice, are some of the subjects wittily and "insouciantly" discussed. Belonging to the same genre are his many essays on such topics as food and drink, fauna and flora, and the art of living in general. The weight of these essays is light if measured in terms of action, described or inspired, but their artistic value as mood pictures and philosophical contemplations on life is very high indeed. Another typical and lengthier example, "Ho ch'a" (Tea Drinking), is translated here as an illustration of these characteristic features of his style and manner.

Tea Drinking

Last time when Hsü Chih-mo lectured in the P'ing-min High School on Tea Drinking—not the settling of disputes over cups of tea that Hu Shih was talking about—I had no time to attend; I also regret not having seen his accomplished lecture notes, but I surmise that he was lecturing on the Japanese Tea Ceremony (translated into English as "Teaism"),[187] and I am sure it must have been a fine talk. The meaning of the tea ceremony, expressed in common language, can be described as "to snatch a relaxed moment in a busy life" and "to create happiness amidst bitterness," or as "to enjoy some little beauty and harmony in this imperfect present world, to comprehend eternity in a short, fleeting moment." It is an art representative of the "symbolistic culture" of Japan. Mr. Hsü no doubt will have given a thorough and ingenious exposition of it, and I need add no more. What I want to talk about here is nothing but my personal, very ordinary tea drinking. In tea drinking, green tea belongs to the orthodox school. Black tea already has no sense and beauty, and is worse even when sugar is added, or even milk! George Gissing's *Private Papers of Henry Ryecroft* [188] is a very interesting book, but when he talks about tea drinking in the Chapter "Winter" he considers the afternoon black tea with buttered bread to be the happiest event in the day of an English family. [He says,] tea drinking has had a history of thousands and hundreds of years in China, yet it seems doubtful whether the Chinese derived even a particle of this [English] pleasure and advantage from it.[189] I definitely disagree with him.

One can of course consume black tea and toast, but this is making a meal of it when one is hungry. The tea drinking that I am talking about is to drink clear tea and appreciate its color, aroma, and flavor, not necessarily to quench a thirst, and less even to fill the stomach. In the olden days the Chinese used to eat roasted tea or ground tea, but nowadays they only infuse tea. Okakura Kakuzō in his *Book of Tea*[190] very ingeniously calls it "naturalistic tea."[191] The important thing for us is the natural excellence of its taste. Chinese go to the tea house and for hours drink one cup after the other, as if just back from the desert, which is very much like my own purpose when I drink tea (I heard in Fukien and Kwangtung that there is something called *kung-fu* [leisure] tea drinking, which of course also has its sense); unfortunately, it has become too foreignized recently and lost its original meaning. As a result, the tea houses have become something like eating places. Only in the countryside is the old style still preserved, but rooms and utensils are extremely simple. However, that may indeed be called the real essence of tea drinking, though one would perhaps not allow that they have achieved the *tao* of tea drinking.

Tea should be had in a place with tiled roof and papered windows, using water from a pure well and green tea, in simple elegant porcelain utensils, in the company of two or three others. Half a day of such relaxation is worth ten years in this world of toil. After having had one's tea, one may return to one's occupation, be it for gain or for fame, but the occasional short relaxation one should on no account do without.

In China, melon seeds are usually eaten with tea, which I don't feel is very fitting. One should eat with one's tea some light, insipid tea tidbits, but the Chinese tea tidbits have become *Man Han po-po*,[192] which are more or less like the *a-a-tou*[193] and not things you eat with your tea. Japanese tea tidbits, though made only of bean and rice, are beautiful in appearance, simple in taste, and therefore qualify well to be eaten with tea, like the various kinds of *yōkan* (Japanese sweetmeats) (which, according to Ueda Kyōsuke's findings,[194] originated in the *yang-kan-ping* of T'ang China),[195] and which also have a special kind of flavor.

In the tea houses south of the Yangtse they have a kind of *kan-ssu* (bean curd strips), which is finely cut strips of dried bean curd, and to which shredded ginger and soy bean are added and boiled in bouillon. This is then sprinkled with sesame oil and served in this fashion to the customers. The profits from these sales go entirely to the waiters. There is one kind of dry bean curd called *ch'a-kan* (tea bean curd), which is made into strips, and which also goes very well with tea. In Nanking, I often had these to eat and was told the best are produced by a priest of a certain Buddhist temple. I sampled them, too, but I forgot what they were like; I only remember the ones from the Chiang T'ien Ko [restaurant?] in Hsiakuan [a suburb of Nanking]. Students had the habit of not eating the *ch'a-kan* immediately when it was served, but to wait until sesame oil was added for a second time and the hot water renewed, and only then to start eating. This was the best way, because if the serving would have been immediately consumed, a second bowl would arrive and there would have been no time for sociabilities. On the other hand, after a third sprinkling with sesame oil, the dishes would be removed right away, faces would flush with anger, the guests would disperse unhappily, and the meaningfulness of the tea [party] would be dissipated.

In my native place [Shaohsing] outside the Ch'ang-an gate, there is a place called San-chiao-ch'iao (Three Foot Bridge)—actually there are no three feet, the "three" appears here only because the bridge spans three arms of a river. At that place there is a bean curd shop called Chou Te Ho, whose *ch'a-kan* is very famous. Ordinary dry bean curd is served one and one-half inch square and up to three *fen* [tenth of an inch] thick, and costs two cash. For the same price, Chou Te Ho's pieces are smaller and thinner, amounting to only half the ordinary ones. They are dark and solid like hardwood slabs. Our house was about two hours walk away from San-chiao-ch'iao, so it was not easy for us to get them. We could get some fried in oil. Every day a man carrying a stove and cauldron on a pole over his shoulder would call out along the streets:

La chiang la	Spicy paste gives spice
ma-yu cha	fried in sesame oil
huang-chiang ch'a	red soy sauce rubbed on
la-chiang t'a	spicy paste brushed on
Chou Te Ho ko wu-hsiang	Chou Te Ho style five-spiced
yu-cha tou-fu kan!	oil-fried dried bean curd!

They were prepared just as explained in the [street-vendor's call]. A bamboo splinter was stuck into one end of the curd, and it cost three cash. Dried bean curd, more or less the size of Chou Te Ho's, but very soft, was the ordinary article. Though they may perhaps not be counted as *ch'a-shih* (tea tidbits), they were nevertheless a fine food made of bean, due to the special way of frying them. Bean curd is really one of the wonderful foodstuffs of the Far East and there are many varieties of it, but it has never found a true understanding in the West, just like tea.

In Japan, rice is soaked in tea, which is then called *chasuke,* and usually accompanied by pickled vegetables and *taku'an* (in Fukien called *huang-t'u lo-po* ["yellow earth radish"]). The recipe was transmitted by the Japanese monk Taku'an; [196] it was brought there from China. It has a pure, bland, and pleasantly fragrant flavor. There are times when the Chinese too eat [rice] that way, however only for the reason that they are either poor or thrifty; seldom will someone purposely seek the inherent flavor in green tea and tepid rice, and that is regrettable.

December, 1924

CHAPTER 6

Chou Tso-jen's Period of Disillusionment and Literary Retirement

THE biographical outline that precedes the body of this study remarked on the continuous harassment to which progressive intellectuals in Peking were subjected by the warlord governments of North China.[1] The reactionary trend reached its peak with the establishment of the Tuan-Ch'i-jui government in 1926 and the incursion of the Manchurian forces under Chang Tso-lin in 1927.[2] During this period, many writers and intellectuals sought the safety of the foreign settlements in Tientsin and Shanghai, or exile abroad, rather than risk incarceration, or worse, in Peking.[3] Chou Tso-jen, too, at one time hid in the house of the Japanese military attaché, because he had received warning that his name was on the list of proscribed leftists.[4] The picture changed very much for the better after the arrival of the Kuomintang forces in North China in 1928, but owing to the tensions emerging within the Kuomingtang, suspicions of persons known to have leftist leanings did not cease, nor was full freedom of expression and criticism restored.[5]

The vexations of this period and the bleak prospects for improvement in the future had a most depressing effect on Chou Tso-jen.[6] Disillusioned about the possibilities of ever achieving political and social progress in China, and discouraged by the animosities of rightists and leftists,[7] he came to the conclusion that there was no other way for a scholarly, self-respecting man than to withdraw from the disappointments and frustrations of the time into the peace and quiet of his studio. "To shut the door and study" was to be the maxim that he proclaimed he would follow henceforth.[8] In the preface to *Yung-jih-chi,* written in February, 1929, he also stated: "As to the events of the day, I will certainly not discuss them hereafter." A continuation of this thought is found in the postscript to *K'u-ch'a sui-pi:* "From now on I must do my best to write good articles, and not concern myself with man's petty affairs but talk about plants, insects, and fish. That is important." "Pi-hu tu-shu lun" (On "Shutting the Door and Studying")[9] was the heading of an essay written in 1928, in which he made known his intention of writing no more on topical questions that could involve him in distasteful controversies. The process of withdrawal seems to have continued over the following years. Conditions in China certainly were not such that they could instill a renewed sense of optimism; in Chou himself, the fervor of youth seems to have spent itself: a mellowing of temper and opinion had set in, and a general decline in literary creativity is noticeable thereafter.

In 1934, Chou wrote two little humorous ditties, which candidly reveal a mood of ennui, worldweariness and fatigue, features which become characteristic of most of his subsequent writings. The poems translate somewhat as follows:

Sentiments on My Fiftieth Birthday [10]

I

In former life a humble monk,[11]
   This time a man of the world,
Who will not change his coat and gown
   For the robe of a follower of Buddha.
Outside, I like to gather tales of ghosts,
   Inside my studio, I paint snakes all day.[12]
As old age comes, I fondly toy with my antiques,
   Or, leisurely content, plant sesame seed.
Ask me not to find the sense in all of this,
   Just join me in my studio for a cup of turbid tea.

II

Half Confucian and half Buddhist,
   Bald of head, yet not "enrobed,"
In middle-age as unconcerned as grass outside my window.
   I make an unconventional living, holed up like a snake.
My vain desire is humbly for a bite of garlic;
   I may also have to slap the table for some crumbs of sesame.[13]
I talk of fox-spirits and ghosts as a normal preoccupation
   But have no time for long polemics.

As soon as these two poems were published in the *Jen-chien-shih* magazine, there was an outcry from the reading public. He was denounced for retiring into an ivory tower; [14] and, in an unflattering sense, he was compared to T'ao Yüan-ming, who too—in the opinion of many—had shirked his public responsibilities by choosing the life of a stay-at-home gardener and farmer. [15] In the Shanghai *Shen-pao,* a critic responded with his own ditty in the same rhyme and rhythm as Chou's:

> Not mingling in the bustling life, a solitary crane,
>> Happy in his cold-blooded detachment, cold as a snake.
> Serving up humorous stories to amuse others,
>> Afraid of involvement, he indulges in nauseating trash. . . .

and ending with:

> If the people are misled, who is to blame?
> He is enraptured with "pure disputations" over cups of tea. [16]

Another critic, writing in 1936, expressed his disdain even more to the point in the following manner:

If we look at Chou Tso-jen these days, we see how he strives to emulate in his writings the vigor of the mature men of the Ming dynasty and their well-tempered perfection, and, while dealing with such trifling topics as plants, insects, fish, and the like, does nothing else but "gaze at the clouds" and "drink turbid tea," [17] in these times when dangers are all around us, then we really feel that Chou Tso-jen, like some prehistorical ancients, [18] has become dispassionate to the extent of not even lifting his hand to scare away the fly on his cheek. Extreme inertia, like a piece of rotten wood! What is left of the memory of his glory! [19]

Two of Chou's old friends tried to vindicate him. Lin Yutang wrote of the warmth that is beneath an outer coldness. [20] Yü Ta-fu admonished his readers not to ignore Chou's continuing guidance in intellectual matters. Yü portrayed Chou as a man in a traffic tower, who shines his red and green lights with a serious purpose when necessary, but at times of leisure plays purposelessly with the colored lights for his own amusement, a harmless gaming at times when no serious need requires his attention. [21] Chou himself was irked and surprised by the response to what he had intended as nothing more serious than amusing and humorous ditties. [22] In his preface to *Tse-hsieh-chi* (1927), he had already laid claim to the epithet of a "Rebel and Recluse" that I. Goldberg had coined for Havelock Ellis.[23] Chou attempted to maintain this image for himself, but his role as an active protagonist of social and literary rebellion could no longer be maintained. His essays after the years 1927–28 become more and more concerned with topics of the past, especially bibliophilic and bibliographic notes on books added to his collection, and even his more contemplative essays become overloaded with quotations and bibliographic references.

The literary productions of his later years are still of great interest, not so much for their social, political, or philosophical purposes, nor for their stylistic perfection, but rather for their importance to the study of Chinese literary history. These essays represent the fruit of his great erudition in the field of Chinese literature and give interesting information on book treasures that he discovered in the famous book markets of Peking, or that he received from friends of similar literary bent. Chou's retreat into the study of older Chinese works must to a considerable extent be attributed to the circumstances of life under the increasing military and political pressures of the Japanese on North China. A preoccupation with books was a device to escape from the unpleasant realities of the political scene and was consistent also with lifelong habits and established cultural traditions. In 1940, he published *Ping-chu-t'an* (Talks by Candlelight), of which the title already suggests reading into the late hours of the evening by the flickering light of a candle. In 1941, a volume of commentaries on books he had read appeared under the title *Yao-t'ang yü lu* (Jottings by Yao-t'ang). Yao-t'ang was one of his pseudonyms. In 1942, a similar collection entitled *Yao-wei-chi* (Bitter Taste Collection) made its appearance. In 1944, *Yao-t'ang tsa-wen* (Random Essays of Yao-t'ang) and *Shu-fang i-chiao* (A Corner of the Library) were published; they contain essays of a similar nature and include commentaries and criticisms on his reading as well as reminiscences of past events and old friends.[24]

After his release from prison in 1949, Chou Tso-jen had to accommodate himself to the much more restrictive regime of the Communists. The role of the independent critic was no longer possible, and what remained for him to do was translate, particularly from his beloved Greek myths,[25] and to reminisce about the life of Lu Hsün, his older, more famous brother, who had in the meantime been enshrined as the literary idol of Chinese communism.

These later writings have their own value, in part because they appear to be comparatively free from politically inspired distortion and embellishment, but also because their interest does not depend upon literary qualities per se but rather upon factual data of historical relevance. These later writings may therefore be left to the literary historian of the life, age, and cult of Lu Hsün for whatever biographical or historical data they may contain.

CHAPTER 7

Conclusion

THE radical changes of the last few decades have little dimmed general public interest in the essays of Chou Tso-jen, though they belong to a past era. This fact is partly due to Chou's technical skill as a writer; to a great extent, his attraction as an essayist also derives from the broad humanitarian content of his writings, a humanitarianism that is valid beyond the limits of space and time. In China, humanitarian ideals have existed since antiquity, and they have found ample expression in her literature. However, in China, as in the rest of the world, periods of emotional imbalance have from time to time beclouded man's vision and blinded him to his very nature. Chou was born toward the end of what he considered one such period, and much of the significance of his work lies in his efforts to bring to an end the "dark" order of modern times and to reassert the values of humanitarianism, the eternally "modern" order of human reason and naturalness.

Three different intellectual and literary traditions can be said to have molded Chou's mind and contributed to his ultimate success: the Chinese tradition to which he was born and in which he grew to young manhood, the cultural tradition of the Meiji-Showa period in Japan, and, lastly, the literary movements of the post-Victorian English revolutionaries and the progressive minds of late nineteenth-century Europe.

Traditional Chinese philosophy and the humanistic values which it fostered made an indelible impress upon his mind. Chou was always ready to admit that he was a *ju-chia,* a Confucian scholar, both by character and conviction, and he gave that term a broad humanitarian meaning. He was gratified to discover that rejuvenation of the national spirit could be based on much in traditional teachings, provided, of course, that these teachings were correctly interpreted. He referred to the Chinese concept of *chung-yung* as a synonym for the Greek sophrosyne, thus designating true humanitarianism as his ideal of a modern Chinese mental outlook.

From Japanese culture, the traditional art forms of the *haiku* and *kyōgen* provided understanding and inspiration, but the most lasting and important influence on his carrier as a modern essayist came from the writings of the realists of the Meiji-Showa era. True, the Japanese themselves had taken example from European models, but they nevertheless constituted important inspirational models in his development as a writer. Foremost in this regard, they demonstrated by example the need, the possibility, and the technique of adapting the forms and ideas of the new European Enlightenment to the Asian scene.

It may be said that Chou served his apprenticeship in modern Western literature; he began his career as a man of letters by translating modern European essayists. Still deeper exploration of Western cultural traditions revealed, when compared to the stale, impersonal, and doctrinaire mannerisms of much Chinese writing of recent centuries, a welter of new ideas worthy of consideration. The honest, uninhibited exploration of natural human emotions which he encountered in contemporary Western literature and philosophy seemed to him, as to many of his time, a revelation of a new and healthy tendency in art, an avenue that his frustrated generation had been seeking. Possessing an open mind and cosmopolitan spirit, the problem of "foreignizing" was not a debatable alternative, but rather an immediate task to be undertaken in the name of spiritual reform, the learning, or relearning of a realistic humanitarianism at the hand of foreign examples. From these diverse sources, a synthesis of Chinese, Japanese, and European values was fashioned, which in turn are reflected in his theories of literature and the standards which he adopted as a writer, translator, and critic. As he reviewed literary developments in his own country,[1] he conceived these developments as representing the interactions between two main schools of thought, the *yen-chih* school and the *tsai-tao* school.[2] The former regarded the main function of literature to be artistic expression of the individual writer's thoughts and emotions, while the latter school insisted that literature was nothing but the vehicle of the *tao,* with the term *tao* here understood in the narrow sense of the Confucianist tradition.

The first generation of modern Chinese writers was in revolt against the neo-Confucianist didacticism of the later Ch'ing period; as one of this young group, Chou saw his own time as signifying a return to the *yen-chih* philosophy in literature. The word "return" is used here with a certain emphasis and purpose, because a second observation made by Chou was that the so-called New Literature of China was in its literary philosophy nothing but a return to the philosophy of the *Kung-an* and *Ching-ling* schools of late Ming times.[3]

The nature of literature he defined as "the beautiful form, in which an author communicates his particular ideas and emotions, so that a reader may gain pleasure from it."[4] The inclusion of the term "pleasure," that is, esthetic enjoyment, in his definition of literature was obviously meant to forestall a purely didactic or utilitarian viewpoint, and to proclaim his unequivocal stand on the side of the *yen-chih* proponents, because only within this school of thought could the humanitarianism and individualism of modern literature hope to flourish and to maintain an unfettered existence. This adherence to the *yen-chih* philosophy of literature, with its insistence on freedom of individual creativity in art and the high value placed on the esthetic element in literature, rather than on the moral that it may preach, brought him rather close to an "art for art's sake" concept of literature. However, for Chou, the humanitarian, man remained the focal point of all things, and humanity as a guiding principle could never be abandoned for an extreme estheticism. Thus, as he once wrote:

The correct interpretation [of the purpose of literature] still sees the ultimate aim in art [i.e., in the esthetic]. However, literary art must pass through the author's emotions and thoughts, and through contacts with life. In other words, it is the author's use of artistic methods to express his emotions and ideas concerning human life, in order to have the reader gain aesthetic enjoyment and interpretation of life. Thus, what we demand is therefore a literature based on a "human life" viewpoint.[5]

This concept of "human life" is further elaborated in the essay "Jen ti wen-hsüeh (Humane Literature), a "crucial document"[6] which is translated in full below, and in the essay "Hsin wen-hsüeh ti yao-ch'iu" (Demands of the New Literature). In the latter, he proclaims that ideally literature must first be human, in contrast to animalistic (i.e., bestial or depraved) in nature, and in contrast to "spirit-natured" (i.e., superhuman or supernatural) literature. Secondly, it must also belong to the human race, that is, include every single human individual, without limiting itself to one particular race, country, district, or family. Another aspect of "humane" literature which he emphasized is that literature must emerge truthfully and honestly from the artist's own personality: "False, imitative, unnatural writings—regardless of age—are all equally of no value, and this is so because they have no real personality." [7] The esthetic and moral requirements of truthfulness do not limit literature to the reporting of actual happenings, but truthfulness must be regarded as a fundamental sincerity and honesty of character and conviction on the part of the author. Myth and folktale, of which Chou was extremely fond, were accorded full literary value in his lexicon. Although not factually true, myth and legend represent, he believed, true expressions of popular beliefs and convictions of one time or another. [8]

The basic truthfulness that he postulated for all literature excluded immediately all literary expression except that created freely and unrestrictedly. On the other hand, he opposed literature produced under the direction or influence of pressure groups or the state itself. He condemned the reactionary warlords in North China of the 1920's for their actions against progressive writers. He was equally disdainful of Marxist regimentation:

The path of literature one must stride by oneself; no teacher can teach it and even less can the masses give directions. Literature that is dictated by those in power, or literature that has perforce to be literature of the fourth estate, or that has to extol the merits of the Sages or the Perfect Way of the ancient Kings, all such literature is equally false. [9]

The term "socialist realism" was not yet in use during that period of his life, but "proletarian literature," the byword of Marxists of the 1930's, was similar in meaning. Chou rejected it, not only for what he regarded as its lack of truthfulness, once it had become subservient to political directives, but also for its direct opposition to his avowed principle of humanitarianism, which admitted no limitations upon art for group or class reasons. He wrote:

I think there cannot be any "classes" within literature, although what is expressed may very well be related to the spirit of a certain class or historical era, and the formal elements may also differ according to contents. At present, it is capitalist thought that permeates upper and lower strata with morals and customs based on the system of private ownership. This is clearly proved, for instance, when one-sided chastity for women, concubinage, and slave-girl ownership are publicly acknowledged and sung about. Now a small minority has risen in opposition. In literature one can observe evidence of this kind of anti-capitalist thought. I don't call it "proletarian" ideology, because I feel it is not a matter of classes, though it has developed simultaneously with the social movement. However, these people are not necessarily motivated by class consciousness; it is only that their mental attitude opposes the traditional capitalist thinking and that makes them rally forth in opposition.[10]

And on another occasion:

Although a writer hopes that the people will understand his art, he must not forcibly accommodate himself to compromise with the people, because it is my opinion that art is after all an expression of the author's emotional life; to make an impression on others is its natural function. If he now were to relinquish his very self and follow others in quest of understanding from a majority, the result would be, at best, an exemplary piece of "pop literature," but not an expression of his real self.[11]

All these statements affirm Chou's belief in art as the free and truthful expression of the human individual. The same high standards are apparent in his activities in the two subsidiary fields in which he achieved prominence in prewar years, namely, the fields of translation and literary criticism. Translations occupy a large portion of Chou's literary production. Here, too, Chou was not only a diligent practitioner, but he also gave thought to the nature and principles of translation. His respect for the individuality and uniqueness of a piece of art made it appear to him almost impossible to re-create an author's work, especially a poem: "Poetry cannot be translated; only the original is a poem. Any further translation is like a schoolmaster's droning out his explanations of T'ang poetry." [12] On the other hand, accomplished and successful translations can become pieces of art in themselves: "I believe translation is half creation; it is also capable of revealing the translator's individuality, because the motivation of any true translation must be a complete resonance between translator and author." [13] Chou's extensive experience and insight into the problems of translation are evident in his essay "T'an fan-i" (Speaking of Translations). The main theme of this essay is that artistic translation presupposes freedom of choice and artistic inspiration, almost equal to that which motivated the original author.

The same strong emphasis on a free and unfettered spirit governed his attitudes toward literary criticism. Imbued with the high principles of humanitarianism, he belittled petty, intolerant fault finding and the arrogance of the average literary critic of his time. A true critic, he believed, was that person who could create a work of art in its own right, a critique reflecting understanding and appreciation of the author's work. In this sense Chou may have been justified in stating, in 1923, that modern literary criticism was nonexistent in China. He explained in his essay "Wen-i p'i-p'ing tsa-hua" (Random Remarks on Literary Criticism) [14] that criticism was generally regarded as almost synonymous with abuse and slander, and that the average critic believed himself to be endowed with the competence and authority to pass judgments according to allegedly objective rules and standards of art. Chou reminded his readers that Mencius, however, had graphically affirmed the imponderable quality of true art,[15] and that T'ao Yüan-ming had also been aware of the sublime art of literary criticism, namely, "to enjoy interesting literature together and to analyze together uncertain meanings." [16] These were the principles which Chou himself supported, but he found his concept of enlightened criticism best enunciated in the writings of Anatole France:

Criticism, like philosophy and history, is a sort of romance designed for those who have sagacious and inquiring minds, and every romance is, rightly taken, an autobiography. The good critic is he who relates the adventures of his own soul among masterpieces. Objective criticism has no more existence than objective art, and all those who deceive themselves into the belief that they put anything but their own personalities into their work are dupes of the most fallacious of illusions.[17]

Chou's humanitarianism, the underlying and guiding philosophy of his literary activities, was modern in nature, and different therefore from the humanitarianism characteristic of earlier Chinese literary history, chiefly because it dealt with the concerns of modern man, and particularly with the spiritual and intellectual concerns of contemporary life. Moreover, it did so in an enlightened and knowledgeable manner. With respect to subject matter and method of treatment, but also in terms of form, style, and language, his essays and related endeavors represent a modern outlook. For instance, in matters of form, Chou showed a strong preference for the essay. One of the characteristics of the essay is its individualism and subjectivism. It presupposes on the part of the writer the conviction that individual, subjective observations and opinions are important, and, in the reader, a desire to experience the individual, subjective contemplations of a fellow human being. Emphatic individualism is the essay's conspicuous mark of modernism.

The style which Chou developed is characteristically modern in its relaxed naturalness, its smoothly flowing and lively language, a language that almost from the beginning was without hesitation closely related to the vernacular. "To write as one speaks" had become a slogan of the day, as well as a pitfall to many who attempted to do so. However, Chou's ability to "write as one speaks," and, at the same time, to impart fluidity and grace to the everyday language helped vindicate the slogan as a workable maxim. To a great extent, it was also due to his choice, and that of many of his contemporaries, of the vernacular as a viable literary language that the fears of the traditionalists were shown to be groundless. The use of a vernacular style at the same time manifested a humanitarian concern for the less privileged who, in the past, would have been precluded from literary enjoyment due to the intricacies of the literary language.

In eulogizing Chou Tso-jen as a pioneer of the essay during the crucial years of modern China's literary development, we are not unaware of the fact that Chou, the man, was as complex a personality as any human being. In fact, many of his beliefs and actions have invited strong criticism, particularly that he twice in his literary career turned his back upon the outside world and his nation's problems, when he might have been expected to give guidance and leadership. Others have criticized his seeming compromise with the Japanese invaders of his homeland. Even his great faith in humanitarianism might often—in times of national crises—have appeared obsolete and anachronistic to many. However, regardless of whatever justification might possibly be found for some of the arguments of his critics and detractors, his positive contributions toward the literary and intellectual progress of his country cannot be ignored. Throughout his active life, and within the sphere of his influence, he did much to advance human progress and to enrich human life. This alone would appear ample vindication for any man's life, regretful though it is that in his case he early ceased to participate actively in public life. We are here reminded of the picture of the torchbearer that Havelock Ellis drew in the Foreword of his *New Spirit:* "The torchbearer drops into the darkness, but he does so only after handing the torch to the runner who comes up from behind and outpaces him in the race towards progress." Chou Tso-jen, too, was a torchbearer for a time in the modernization of his country and in the crucial, formative years of modern Chinese letters.

Appendix

Getting Oneself Hurt [1]

Once I had the plan of getting myself steel armor covered with spikes, each spike two inches longer than the longest tooth of a wild animal. With this armor I could roam about in the wilderness without fear of animal attack. If they should attack, I could just imitate a wild chestnut, or coil up like a porcupine and remain quiet. The animals would be unable to do anything to me. Without moving a hand, I would let them hurt themselves and run away.

In the Buddhist sutras there is mention of snakes of different poisons, the worst being the poison-by-sight snake, because a person would be poisoned and die by merely looking at the snake. In the early Ch'ing dynasty, Chou An-shih,[2] commenting on the *Yin-chih-wen,*[3] said: "The two snakes that Sun Shu-ao [4] killed were probably of this type of poison-by-sight snake, because by looking at the snakes he was about to die." (Actually the snakes may perhaps only have been ill-omened animals, like the owl.) Later he says there are still such snakes living in Hunan, but they are not a bit poisonous anymore.

When I was small, I read the tales of knight-errants [5] in the T'ang dynasty collectanea and these stories scared me very much. The knight-errants were all men who by ascetic practice had attained the *tao,* but their tempers were very vile. For no apparent reason they would send a sword flying over a hundred paces through the air to cut a man's head off. Then there were the warrior-saints; they were even worse. Their flying swords would swish through the air like a streak of bright light, pursuing their aim for over ten miles and not stopping until blood stained the blade. When I read that, I prayed in my heart that I would never meet a warrior-hero, for fear that with one little carelessness I might cause offense.

A few days ago the newspapers reported that outside the Hsin Hua Gate [6] some teachers, staff members, and students "got themselves hurt." Everybody was puzzled by such extraordinary happenings but, looking at it as the old romanticist that I am, I cannot see anything extraordinary in it at all. In this world of ours anything may happen. That is what brought to mind the three stories mentioned above, and I certainly feel that "getting oneself hurt" is quite possible and within reason. To anyone doubting me and my romantic tales, I can furnish more facts in proof.

Three, four years ago a small passenger ferry between Pukow and Hsiakuan got itself stuck on the prow of a Chinese warship anchored in mid-stream. The ferry immediately sank, but according to reports no passengers were lost. (Presumably they had registered them one by one when going on board, so that there were records to check.)[7]

One or two years later a China Merchant Co. ship on the Yangtse got itself stuck on the prow of another warship, which happened to carry the incumbent President of the Republic. The merchant vessel immediately sank and a number of worthless people lost their lives. I don't remember anymore the time, the names of the ships, or the number killed; I only remember there was a memorial service in Shanghai and one of the funerary scrolls read:

> Not necessarily all on the same boat were enemies,
> Unexpectedly, we too have become exalted.[8]

It is therefore clear that "getting oneself hurt" is a frequent occurrence in China. The full responsibility in such cases must, of course, rest with the party that gets hurt. For instance, if I should wear spiked armor, or if someone should look at the poison-by-sight snake, or if I were a warrior-saint and someone should push me, look at me, or offend me, and if as a result someone should get hurt, how could you say it was my fault? Moreover, take fire, for instance; it can light up darkness, cook food, but if not extinguished, it can burn down the house and harm people. If a child ignorant of fire's usefulness, should stick his hand into it and get burnt, that would naturally be the child's own fault.

I heard the present incident of "getting oneself hurt" resulted from petitioning. I can't keep from blaming again those that got hurt; I have always felt this method is wrong. The custom of presenting petitions is—temporarily and perforce—still prevalent in countries that have only recently adopted constitutions; it is out of use in all other places. For instance, in Russia in nineteen hundred and something, only because of an incident of people wanting to present a petition, it happened that the guards at the Winter Palace opened fire and people got hurt much more badly.[9] But from then on they did not petition anymore.—

I hope Chinese petitioning will also stop henceforth; everyone exert yourself, each on his own!

June 1921 at Hsishan.

Candy Selling

There is a paragraph in chapter two of the *Nien-t'ang shih-hua* by Ts'ui Hsiao-lin,[10] which reads:

> According to the *Jih-chih-lu*,[11] the candy vendor in olden days blew a flute; nowadays, he beats a gong. I found in Hsü Ch'ing-ch'ang's poem [the phrase]: "Sounding the gong to sell 'night candies,'" proof that in Ming times candy vendors sounded gongs.

Note: the five characters "ch'iao lo mai yeh t'ang" are contained in volume four of the *Hsü Wen-ch'ang chi*,[12] the mention of Ch'ing-ch'ang is a mistake for Ch'ing-t'eng or Wen-ch'ang. The heading of the original poem is T'an-yang;[13] it is in ten sections of which the fifth reads:

> What was it that moved India
> Unexpectedly to be in T'ai-ts'ang?
> Oh, how marvellous to listen to the White Buddha!
> Having dreamt [a dream of transitory glory] that
>   lasted only as long as it takes to cook
>   yellow millet,[14]
> I am now begging for food in the morning,
> And beat the gong to sell "night candy."

The topic of this song is of course the story of the daughter of Wang Hsi-chueh,[15] but parts of the poem are difficult to explain. However, I need only the last phrase to prove the selling of "night candy."

There is not a word about it in the section on foods in the *Yüeh-yen*;[16] there is even nothing about *li-kao-t'ang* (pear sweetmeat), which is rather disappointing. If there were no "night candies" in Shaohsing, how much duller would life be for the little ones, because this candy and *chih-kao* (toasted pastry) are two great favorites with the children; they all have to have them, whether street urchins or the children of the rich. The name "night candy" cannot be explained; it is just a round, hard candy, also commonly called "longan candy," because it looks like the longan fruit. There are also some with pointed corners, which are called *tsung-tzu-t'ang* (candy like Dragon Boat Festival dumplings) some red, some yellow, and each used to cost one cash. At the larger street-corner candy store, you might have gotten ten candies for seven or eight cash, but this was the price thirty years ago, which I am sure must have greatly changed. The *li-kao-t'ang* cost four cash each and ordinary children would hardly ask for them. There were also others that could be had for one cash, namely, *ch'ieh-fu* (dried eggplant?) and mei-ping (plum pastry). The eggplants were boiled with granulated sugar, then dried outdoors and sold by weight. But the vendors cut them into suitable lengths and there were bound to be longer and shorter pieces, so the children would pick the heaviest. That was the *ch'ieh-fu*. The *mei-ping* were prepared by boiling plums with liquorice root. This was then pounded into a pulp, together with the kernels, and patterned into round cookies the size of a newly minted copper-cent piece. To suck them was especially delicious, like *ch'ing-yen* plums (pickled green plums).

The candy vendors mostly used to carry their wares by means of bamboo poles, but not over the shoulder. It was actually only a basket called *chiao-lan* (lift-up basket) in the local dialect. The upper part had wooden boxes filled with different kinds of candy and a glass cover over it. They had wooden tressels, like folding chairs, to put the basket on, when waiting for customers. When they moved on, they would fold it up and pin it under their right arm, while the left arm would hold the basket; this was called *chiao* (lift-up) in the local dialect. The free left hand would hold a small gong and the right hand a wooden tablet shaped like a *hu* (audience tablet). They would hit the gong and cry out "tang, tang," which was then the signal of the candy seller. When the children heard it, they would all get excited, almost like the fair ladies who get stirred by the drum of the ladies-goods vendor.

The gong was quite different from other gongs. It had a diameter of less than a foot, a narrow rim and no strings. When hitting it, one finger would press against the inner rim, completely different from the brass gongs that are held by a string and hit with a stick. The people used to call it a *t'ang-lo* gong, the "t'ang" pronounced as in the word for soup, in the fourth tone, indicating the sound that it gave off. Although it was certainly also a metal gong, it was quite different from the gongs mentioned in novels when it says: "and the gong was sounded to order the troops to fall back." Ku T'ing-lin[17] was right in saying that the candy vendors in his days beat gongs. If the expression has been used in too general a way, such as is unavoidable in *ku-wen* (classical literary language), it must not be held against Ku.

The sellers of *chih-kao* (toasted pastry) came mostly in the afternoon. They had a fire going in a bamboo crate, with a cooking pot on the fire. Pastry made of brown sugar and rice flour was cut into bits and roasted; each piece cost one cash. They also had *ma-tz'u* (pastry) and would call out loudly: "Ma-tz'u ho chih-kao." The word "ho" was only an expletive, like the "ho ho" of old man Hsiao,[18] but in Chekiang dialect it was more guttural than anywhere else. In the morning, there were others selling painted pastry. On the pastry some propitious words were printed in red characters in relief. There were also many other kinds, like *ts'ai-t'ang-kao, fuling-kao, kuei-hua nien-kao* (pastries), etc., but they called them out merely as *kao-ho*. It seems they served as breakfast for the grown-ups, not like the *chih-kao* (toasted pastry) that were eaten by children.

Since I came to Peking I have not seen these pastries anymore, because in the South rice is the staple food and these pastries were made of rice flour; the situation is completely different [in the North].

The things we ate when we were small were not always so tasty but later they seem to become extremely delicious and unforgettable. This is exactly the reason why I keep remembering all these candies and sweetmeats.

Some years ago I read *Sentetsu sōdan* by the Japanese Hara Kōdō.[19] In the third volume some paragraphs deal with Chu Shun-shui,[20] and one part reads:

> Shun-shui had become quite assimilated throughout these years. He could speak Japanese; however, when he fell seriously ill, he talked again in his native tongue and none of the servants could understand him. (The original text is in Chinese writing.)

I felt a great pity when I read this. The language that Shun-shui spoke must have been the dialect of Yü-yao. Although I am from the neighboring district, I can understand that dialect and would have understood him. Yü-yao also has the "night candies" and *chih-kao* (toasted pastry). It is a pity that Shun-shui did not mention them, probably because nobody would have understood him anyhow. But then I also think of the *T'ao-an meng-i* and regret that these (pastries and candies) have also not been mentioned.

Random Notes, Peking, February 25, 1938.

Addendum: The *Yüeh-yen* does not mention candies but reports briefly on pastries. For instance, under *yin-kao* (painted pastries) it comments:

> From rice flour, made into squares, on top letters printed with colored flour. Are used as gifts, together with *man-t'ou* (dumplings) for weddings and birthdays.

Furthermore, under *ma-tz'u* it comments:

> Glutinous rice flour, filling of red bean (paste), like cookies, toasted and eaten, sold by carrier-vendors. If eaten in excess, can cause death.

The last words are rather superfluous, because someone had once made a wager [as to how many *ma-tz'u* he could eat] and had died as a result of it. Fan has written this as a warning, but actually it does not apply only in the case of *ma-tz'u*. If *Chi-ku-t'ou kao-kan* (chicken bone dry) pastry is eaten in excess, it is also harmful.

In observing the peculiarities of a locality, its foods are very important. Not only its everyday staple foods, but also the tidbits and sweets are very interesting. It is a pity that few people have given these things their attention. The literati, native to the district, consider these things too trivial to talk about; outsiders give only slight attention to foods, but instead write about men and women, producing such books as the *Hsien-hua Yang-chou*.[21] Actually, the affairs of men and women are more or less the same and not worth that much effort. On the other hand the various foodstuffs are full of "flavor" and could be talked about much more. Added on the 28th.

Our Own Garden

One hundred and fifty years ago, Voltaire of France wrote his novel *Candide,* in which he described the calamities of this world and ridiculed the paradisical philosophies of Dr. Pangloss. After a great deal of suffering, Candide and his old master Dr. Pangloss settle in a corner of Turkey and finally find a peaceful existence cultivating their garden. With regard to Dr. Pangloss' philosophies of paradise, Candide utters the following conclusion: "They are all very well, but the best is still for each to cultivate his own garden." This maxim has become a standing phrase in common usage. The meaning is also very clear and does not require my footnotes, but if I now copy it down here, I have yet another meaning in mind.

The expression "one's own garden" actually has a very broad meaning; it is not limited to any one kind of thing; one may grow fruits or vegetables, or medicinal herbs, or roses and violets.[22] As long as one follows one's own inclination, stays on one's acknowledged piece of land, be it large or small, and exerts one's strength in growing [a crop], that would completely fulfil one's natural duties.

With all these plain and ordinary words, what I want to declare here especially is only that growing roses and violets would also constitute cultivating one's garden. Compared to growing fruit, vegetables, and medicinal herbs, these would only be different species, but they would be equally valuable.

Our own garden is literature; I want to state this here in advance. I do not at all resent or look down upon other activities. I ordinarily acknowledge that all kinds of activities are necessary for life. Actually, it is to a smaller extent due to not having that kind of talent and to a larger extent due to a lack of that kind of interest, that of all [human activities] I must concentrate on this one pursuit. But, I do not regret my choice; I am definitely not lamenting the fact that the acreage is small and the harvest poor, and, seemingly, also of no usefulness. To follow one's heart's avocation in growing roses and violets is the right thing to do, out of respect for one's individuality. If some say that a person must, in due course, repay his debt to society, I believe I have already done so, because society does not need only fruits, vegetables, and medicinal herbs, but it needs roses and violets equally urgently. Any society that despises them [roses and violets] must be completely demented; it is a society in form only, a society without spiritual life, and one we need not take into consideration. If, under certain pretexts, man is forced to give up his individuality in the service of a demented society, or, expressing the same thing in more beautiful language, if concessions are to be made to the mentality of such a society, that would be as unreasonable as using the pretext of the *lun ch'ang* (social relationships prescribed by Confucianism) to enforce loyalty to an overlord, or to make people fight in the name of a country.

Some may say that according to my words I am advocating the art of the "human life" school. Generally speaking, I have of course no objections to "human life" art; but, what is commonly referred to as the "human life" school proposes an art for life's sake, and, regarding this, I have some opinion.

"Art for Art's Sake," to separate art and life and then to make life an adjunct of art, going even so far as Wilde in advocating that life be made into an art, is certainly not very appropriate. "Art for Life's Sake," to make art an adjunct of life, to make art a tool in improving life, but not an end purpose in itself, does this in any way separate art from life? I, of course, consider art to be "of human life," because it is in fact an expression of our emotional life. How can one possibly separate it from life? "For Life's Sake," to be of benefit to life, is of course one of the basic functions of art, but it is not its only duty. Generally speaking, art is independent. However, it is basically of human nature, therefore, even though it must not be separated from life, it must also not be made servile to human life; just let it be the expression of this complex life, that is all!

The "For Art's Sake" school makes the individual the handicraftsman of art. The "For Life's Sake" school makes art the servant of life; in that way, the individual is the master, he expresses emotions and ideas and [thereby] creates art, and this then becomes part of his life. At the start he does not create for the welfare of others, but when others come into contact with his art, they experience a kind of empathy and elation that fills and enriches their spiritual life, thereby providing a foundation for their real life. That is the crucial point in "human life" art, it has independent, artistic beauty and formless benefits.

The growing of roses and violets, of which I spoke, is just like that: Some grow flowers for their amusement, others grow them with the idea of selling them for money; the real grower of flowers considers growing flowers his life, and yet flowers will nevertheless be beautiful and will nevertheless bring benefit to mankind.

Humane Literature

The New Literature that we must now promote may be expressed in one simple term, "humane literature," and what we must reject is the opposite, the "inhumane literature."

"New" and "old" are really inadequate terms; actually, according to the principle that there is "nothing new under the sun," we can only speak of "right" and "wrong," but not of "new" and "old." If we use the term "new" [in "New Literature"], then we use it to mean "newly discovered," but not "newly invented." The New Continent was discovered by Columbus in the 15th century, but the land had already been there from all antiquity. Electricity was discovered by Franklin in the 18th century, but the phenomenon had also already existed all along. Not that earlier men could not have perceived it, it only so happened that Columbus and Franklin were finally the first to discover the facts. It is the same with the discovery of a truth. Truth always exists without any limitations in time; it is only because of our own ignorance, in being so late to perceive the truth, and being still near the time of its discovery, that we call it "new." Actually it is of extreme antiquity, the same as the New Continent or electricity, it was always in the world and it would be a great mistake to regard it as new as a fresh fruit, or a new dress made to the fashion of the day.

For instance, when we now speak of humane literature, does this phrase not also sound like something new-fashioned? But doing so would be ignoring the fact that as soon as human beings came into existence in this world, humaneness was born. Unfortunately, man was ignorant and persistently would not give heed to humanity's will to walk this correct path, but rather strayed along the paths of animals and ghosts, wandering about aimlessly for many years until finally achieving his emergence. He is like a man who, in bright daylight, has covered his eyes and has blindly dashed about, only to discover, when he finally opens his eyes, that there is good sunlight in this world. Actually, the sun had been enlightening the world all along like this for an immeasurable length of time.

In Europe, the truth of this humaneness was discovered for the first time in the 15th century, resulting in two developments: the religious revolution and the renaissance in art. A second time, it produced the great French Revolution; for a third time it will probably lead to as yet unknown future developments after the European War. The discovery of women and children however emerged only as late as the 19th century; the old traditional position of woman was merely that of man's chattel and slave. In the Middle Ages, the Church was still debating whether woman had a soul and whether woman was to be considered human!

Children, too, used to be nothing but their parents' property. A child was not recognized as a human being that had not yet fully matured, but was taken as a complete man in miniature, [an attitude] which resulted in innumerable domestic and educational tragedies. Only after Froebel [23] and Mrs. Godwin [24] did the light break through; at present, research is being instituted in two great fields, the study of children and the women's question, and one can hope that results will be of the best.

In China, investigations of these questions must start right from the beginning. [Here] the problem of man has heretofore never been solved, not to mention the problems of women and children. If we now make our first step and begin to discuss man, if, after he has been living for over four thousand years, we still investigate the meaning of man, if we try to rediscover him, "clear the 'man' jungle," this has something of the ridiculous in it. However, learning in old age is always one grade better than not learning at all. It is in this sense that we hope, starting out from literature, we will promote some of the ideas of humanitarianism.

Prior to discussing humane literature, we should first clarify the term "human." The human being that we want to deal with is not the so-called "crowning piece of nature," nor the "round skull, square footed" man, but rather the "human species, as it has progressively evolved from the animal kingdom." There are two points of importance here: 1) the evolution has taken place FROM ANIMAL, and 2) man has PROGRESSED from animal.

We acknowledge that man is a living being which, in its outward signs of life, does not differ at all from other living beings. We therefore believe that all man's vital faculties [being naturally endowed] are beautiful and are good, and should find their complete satisfaction. Anything contrary to human nature, unnatural customs and institutions, should all be condemned and amended.

Expressed in other words, these two important aspects constitute the dual nature of man's life: the spirit and the body. Men of old thought that the two primary elements in man's nature, the spirit and the body, existed simultaneously and were in eternal conflict with each other. The bodily element is that which had come down from man's original animal nature. The spiritual was [seen as] the beginning of man's divine nature. The purpose of man's life was viewed as being predominantly the development of his divine nature. The method [to achieve this] was to sacrifice the body for the salvation of the soul. Old traditional religions, therefore, all rigorously enforce asceticism and by various strenuous efforts oppose man's natural instincts. On the other hand, there were the epicureans, who had no regard for the soul, and saw the end merely as a "when I die, bury me" [i.e., "Death is the end of all"]. Both these two parties reached extremes and cannot be said to have shown man the correct way of life. Only in modern times have people realized that the spirit and the body are basically two facets of one thing, and not two primary elements in opposition. The animal nature and the divine nature jointly constitute man's nature. The English 18th century poet Blake [25] has expressed it excellently in his *Marriage of Heaven and Hell:*

(1) Man has no Body distinct from his Soul, for that called Body is a portion of Soul discernible by the five Senses,
(2) Energy is the only life, and is from the Body, and Reason is the bound or outward circumference of Energy.
(3) Energy is Eternal Delight.

Although his words have the flavor of mysticism, they very well express the essential idea of the unity of the spirit and the body. What we believe to be the right way of life for mankind is just this life of a unison of spirit and body. If we refer to man as having progressively evolved from the animal, it is nothing else but indicating in other words that in this man, spirit and body are in [harmonious] unison.

What would be an ideal life for this kind of man? First of all, mutual relations among humanity should be improved. All men constitute humanity and each is but one unit of humanity. Therefore, man should live a life of benefiting self while also benefiting others, and of benefiting others while also benefiting himself. Firstly, regarding the material things of life, each should exert himself to the utmost of human strength and each should get what is humanly necessary. In other words, each man should obtain adequate clothing, food, shelter, medical care and medicine, in exchange for his physical or mental labors, so that he will be able to sustain a healthy life. Secondly, regarding his moral life, the four elements of love, wisdom, trust, and courage shall be its basic morality; all traditional sub-human or ultra-human rules of society should be eliminated, so that every person may enjoy a free and genuinely happy life. Realization of such a humane, ideal life would actually benefit every single person on earth. Although the rich feel they would inevitably have to lose their so-called status, they would thereby obtain salvation from an "inhuman" life, to become perfect human beings; would that not be the utmost of blessings? We may really call this the Gospel of the 20th century, and only regret that few people know of it and that immediate realization is not possible. We shall therefore promote it in the field of literature, and thereby make our humble contribution towards this idea of humanity.

However, it still has to be explained that what I call humanitarianism is not charity as referred to in such common sayings as "have pity and commiserate the people," [26] or "wide generosity and relief of distress among the masses." [27] It is rather an individualistic ideology of basing everything on man. The reasons are:

(1) Within humanity, a man is just like one tree in a forest. If the forest thrives, the single tree in it will also thrive. But if we want the forest to thrive, we have to care for each single tree.
(2) The individual loves humanity because he is one unit of it and because of its relationship to him. Mo-tzu [28] gave as his reason for all-embracing love the fact that "I am within humanity," which is penetratingly expressed. It has the same meaning as the above-mentioned benefiting self by benefiting others, and benefiting others through benefiting oneself.

The humanitarianism that I have in mind therefore starts with man, the individual. To be able to discuss humaneness, love of humanity, one must first have acquired the qualifications of man and stand in the position of man. Jesus said: "Love your neighbor as you love yourself." If you don't love yourself, how would you know to love others "as you love yourself"? As to love without personal involvement, purely for the sake of someone else, I consider this impossible. It is possible that man sacrifices himself for the person *he* loves, or the idea *he* believes in, but acts like cutting off a piece of your flesh to feed an eagle, or perhaps giving your body to a hungry tiger to devour, would constitute ultra-human morality, something that human beings cannot do.

Writing that applies this humanitarianism in its statements and in its studies of all questions concerning human life, that is what we call humane literature, which can be again divided into two kinds:

(1) the principal kind: description of the ideal life, or writings on the heights of advancement attainable by men, and
(2) the secondary kind: descriptions of man's ordinary life, or his inhuman life, which can also contribute toward the purpose of the study.

The largest amount of writing is of the latter kind and it is also the more important, because it enables us to understand the true circumstances of man's life, to point out how it differs from the ideal life, and to devise methods of improvement. Within this category, descriptions of the inhuman life [that some men are forced to lead] are very frequently mistaken by people for "non-human" literature, but actually there is a big difference. For instance, the Frenchman Maupassant's *Une vie* is humane literature about the animal passions of man; China's *Jou-p'u-t'uan*,[29] however, is a piece of non-human literature. The Russian Kuprin's novel *Jama* is literature describing the lives of prostitutes, but China's *Chiu-wei-kuei*[30] is non-human literature. The difference lies merely in the different attitudes conveyed by the works, one is dignified and one is profligate, one has aspirations for human life, and therefore feels grief and anger in the face of inhuman life, while the other is complacent about inhuman life, and the author even seems to derive a feeling of satisfaction from it, and in many cases to deal with his material in an attitude of amusement and provocation. In one simple sentence: the difference of humane and "non-human" literature lies in the attitude which informs the writing, whether it affirms human life or inhuman life. This is the crucial point. The content or the method of writing are of no importance. For instance, stories that advocate that women be buried with their dead husbands, that is, commit suicide rather than remarry, don't they, on the surface, voice "maintenance of customs and ethics?" But forcing people to commit suicide is exactly what constitutes inhuman morality; such writings are therefore non-human literature. In the literature of China, in fact, there has been extremely little humane literature. Almost none of the writings emanating from the Confucian or Taoist schools can qualify. Let us cite examples only from the field of pure literature:

(1) profligate, pornographic books,

(2) books on demons and gods (*Feng-shen-chuan, Hsi-yu-chi*, etc.),

(3) books on immortals (*Lu-yeh hsien-tsung*, etc.),

(4) books on supernatural appearances (*Liao-chai-chih-i, Tzu-pu-yü,* etc.),

(5) books dealing with slavery (Group A with topics: emperors, *chuang-yüan*, prime-ministers; Group B with topics: sacred and divine fathers and husbands),

(6) books on banditry (*Shui-hu-chuan, Ch'i-hsia wu-i, Shih-kung-an,* etc.),

(7) books on men of talent and beautiful women (*San-hsiao-yin-yüan,* etc.),

(8) books of low class humor (*Hsiao-lin kuang-chi*, etc.),[31]

(9) scandal literature,

(10) the old dramas, in which we find all the above ideas crystallized into one.

All these categories of literature are a hindrance to the growth of human nature; they are things that destroy the peace and harmony of mankind; they are all to be rejected. Naturally, this type of literature is extremely valuable in the study of national psychology. Literary criticism may also find some of them admissible [as literature], but from an ideological point of view, all are to be rejected. We do not object to persons of good sense and maturity reading these books. We should heartily welcome it if they would study and criticize them for this would be of great value to the world.

Humane literature must take humane morality as its basis. This question of morality is very broad and cannot be dealt with in detail at once. I only want to mention here a few aspects that have a bearing on literature.

Take for instance love between the sexes; here we have two propositions: 1) equal status for both sides, men and women, and 2) marriage based on mutual love. Works of world literature that have expounded these ideas are among the most excellent pieces of humane literature. For instance Ibsen's plays *A Doll's House, The Lady from the Sea,* the Russian Tolstoy's novel *Anna Karenina,* the Englishman Hardy's novel *Tess,* etc., are all of this nature. The origin of love, according to the Norwegian scholar Westermarck, is "man's liking for what gives him pleasure." The Austrian Lucka then added that love became an exalted emotion because of the many years that the moral nature of man had progressively developed. True love and the life of the two sexes has therefore also this unison of the spiritual and the physical. However, due to the oppressive circumstances and powers of today's society, the emphasis has unavoidably shifted most commonly to one side. This, then, should be stated and studied on the basis of humanitarianism, but we must not extol nor propagate this [one-sidedly physical] life as happy or divine or sacred. I need not even mention Chinese profligate, pornographic literature, but I find equally unacceptable the asceticism of the old Christian Church.

There is also the Russian writer Dostoyevski, a great author of humanitarian literature, who in one of his novels describes how one man loves a woman, who later falls in love with another man, but in devious ways and with great effort the first man causes them [the second man and the woman] to be united. Although Dostoyevski's own words and actions are always consistent, we can never accept the fact that these various actions [described in the story] are compatible with human feelings and with human capabilities; we therefore should not advocate such actions.

Another case is the Indian poet Tagore, who in his novels continuously sings the praises of Eastern thought. In one story he records the life of a widow and describes her *suttee* of the heart (*suttee* is the custom of self-immolation of a widow on the funeral pyre of her husband). In another story he describes how a man forsakes his wife and remarries in England, and how his [Indian] wife even sells her jewelry to keep supporting the husband forever.

If a person is free of body and mind, and from free choice binds himself in love to another person, and then, upon reaching the time when death parts them, will give up his own life, this might indeed be called a matter of morality. But the whole affair must spring from free determination. An act brought about under pressure of despotic traditional rules of society is an altogether different matter. The Indian human sacrifice, the *suttee*, as everybody knows, is an inhuman custom, already recently forbidden by the British. The *suttee* of the heart is merely a variant form of it. One amounts to capital punishment, one to life imprisonment. To speak in Chinese terms: one is *hsün chieh* (to commit suicide rather than remarry), and the other is *shou chieh* (to remain unmarried after the death of the husband).[32] The Sanscrit word *suttee*, I am told, originally had the meaning "chaste woman." Because Indian women have suffered *suttee* for thousands of years, they have nurtured this perverted form of chastity. Those who expound "Easternization" may consider it a valuable national characteristic, while in fact it is merely the evil fruit of an unnatural custom.

The Chinese, for instance, have become accustomed to kowtowing. When they meet, they will for no particular reason salute each other by folding their hands and bowing deeply, all as if they should prostrate themselves before each other. Can we call this the admirable virtue of politeness? If we see such perverted types of so-called morality, it is like seeing a man raised in a pickle-jar with a body like a carrot. We would only feel horror, revulsion, pity, and hate, but would certainly not hold him up for emulation, or voice our approbation.

Next then, there is the love between parents and children. The men of old said: "Love between parents and children has its source in natural disposition." This is well said. Because it is originally indeed a natural love, there would seem to be no need for people to apply binding obligations to it, impeding its growth. If one said that parents beget children because of selfish lust, people may perhaps consider [parenthood] something immoral. It is therefore much more appropriate to define it as arising from "natural disposition." Considering it on the basis of biological fact, parents indeed beget children out of a natural desire. When there is sex life, there will naturally follow propagation of life and efforts to raise one's young; this is the same with all living creatures. When it comes to man, with his greater consciousness of the blending harmony of love and the continuation of one's kind [in the children], there is an even deeper relationship between parents and children. What intelligent people have recently said about the rights of children and the duties of parents are merely deductions from this natural principle, and [as such] nothing new. As to ignorant parents, who look on their children as property to be raised like cattle and horses, that are eaten or ridden at one's convenience when they will have grown big, they show a retrograde misconception. The English educationalist Gorst calls such parents "ape-like degenerates," which is truly no exaggeration.

The Japanese Tsuda Sōkichi in his *Study of National Thought in Literature*,[33] volume 1, says:

> An attitude of filial piety that is not based on love of the parents for their children contravenes common biological fact that elders exist for their offspring, and the factual conditions of human society, namely, that man labors for the future. If one were even to assume that offspring exist for their elders, such kind of morality obviously contains elements of the unnatural.

The elders exist for their offspring. It therefore stands to reason that parents should love and treasure their children, and the children should in turn love and respect their parents. This is a natural fact; it is also a natural disposition. We find literary expression of the love between parents and children most beautifully conveyed in the Greek Homer's epic, the *Iliad*, and in Euripides' tragedy *Troiades*, in the two chapters where Hector is taken by death from his wife and his children.

Recently, Ibsen's *Gengagere* (Ghosts), the German Sudermann's play *Heimat*, the Russian Turgenev's novel *Fathers and Sons*, etc. are all deserving of our study.

As to such cruel superstitious acts as those of a Kuo Chü, who buried his son,[34] and of Ting Lan, who carved the wooden image,[35] we should, of course, cease to praise or propagate such. Cutting out a piece of one's flesh [to feed the parents][36] is merely a residue of [belief in] witchcraft and cannibalism; it can of course not be considered moral, and we should never again permit [such themes] to get into our literature.

From the above, it will have become generally clear what kind of literature we should promote and what kind we should reject. However, we must still add a few words on the matter of old versus new, Chinese versus foreign, to forestall some misunderstandings.

On literature that is opposed to our ideology, we should not, like Hu Chih-t'ang[37] and Ch'ien Lung,[38] write treatises to bring them down by abuse, one by one, old and new, merely according to our own personal viewpoint. If we establish our theory, it shall incorporate only this one viewpoint: the viewpoint of our age. Criticism and proposals shall be two separate things again. In criticizing the writings of the old, we have to realize their time and age, to correctly evaluate them and allot them their rightful position. In propagating our own proposals we must also realize our time and age. We cannot compromise with opposite ideas. For those, we have only one way, namely, to reject them. For instance, in primeval times only primeval ideas prevailed, and witchcraft and cannibalism were then a matter of course. Songs and stories about these customs are therefore still worthwhile studying to increase our knowledge. However, if anyone in modern society would still want to practice witchcraft or cannibalism, he would just have to be seized and confined in a mental hospital.

Next, regarding the question of Chinese versus foreign, we should also firmly embrace the viewpoint of our time and age, and not stake out other boundaries. Geographically and historically, there are indeed many differences, but communications have improved and the [intellectual] atmosphere spreads fast. Mankind can hope to move gradually closer together, and people of one age will live together and exist together. The unit is I, the individual, the sum-total is all humanity. One should not think of oneself as different from the mass of mankind, or as superior in morality, and draw up borders and spheres, because man is always related to mankind and *vice versa*.

If a Chang and a Li are suffering, and [somewhere else] a Peter and a John are suffering, and if I maintain that it is a matter of no concern to me, then my indifference applies to all equally. If I maintain that it is of concern to me, then I am equally concerned in all cases. In detail, this means that although the Changs and the Lis, the Peters and the Johns may have names and nationalities different from my own, they are all in the same way units of mankind, all equally endowed with emotions and natural dispositions. What one of them feels as pain must also be painful to me. The misfortune that befalls one of them can certainly also befall me. Because mankind's fate is one and the same, the anxiety about my own fate should therefore also be anxiety about the common fate of mankind. That is why we should speak only of our time and age and not distinguish between Chinese and foreign. In our occasional creations, we naturally tend toward the Chinese, which we can understand more accurately. Beyond that we must introduce and translate foreign writings in large quantities, extend the mind of the reader, so that he can perceive humanity as a whole, and we must nurture a humane morality and achieve realization of a humane life.

Notes and References

Chapter One

1. Extensive bibliographical data are contained in several of the works listed in the bibliography appended below. A comprehensive account of his life up to 1939 is contained in Matsueda Shigeo's essay "Shu Saku-jin sensei," which is to be found in *Shu Saku-jin bungei zuihitsu shō* (A Collection of Chou Tso-jen's Literary Essays) (Tokyo, 1940), pp. 283–329. Among Chou's own essays, the following contain substantial biographical information: "Chiu jih-chi ch'ao" (From an Old Diary), "Chou Tso-jen tzu shu" (Autobiography), "Wo hsüeh kuo-wen ti ching-yen" (My Experience in Studying Chinese Literature), "Kuan-yü chin-tai ti san-wen" (On Modern Essay Writing), "Wo ti tsa-hsüeh" (The Miscellany of My Knowledge), and "Kuan-yü Lu Hsün" (About Lu Hsün).

Another source of biographical data, particularly as to family background and early youth, is the large volume of Lu Hsün literature, most important being William R. Schultz, "Lu Hsün, the Creative Years," unpubl. diss. (Seattle, Univ. of Washington, 1955), as well as Lu Hsün's own essays "Tzu-chuan" (Autobiography) and "Chao-hua hsi-shih" (Morning Flowers Picked at Evening), *Lu Hsün ch'üan-chi* (The Complete Works of Lu Hsün) (Shanghai, 1948), Vol. XX and II, respectively.

2. Chou Hsia-shou, *Lu Hsün ti ku chia* (Lu Hsün's Old Home) (Hong Kong, 1958), p. 111; also in a letter addressed to Chiang Shao-yüan and entitled "Li ti wen-t'i" (Questions of Propriety), *Yü-ssu*, No. 3 (December, 1924), and particularly the chapter entitled "The Chou Family" in W. Schultz, *op. cit.*, pp. 1-12.

3. Chou Hsia-shou, *op. cit.*, p. 56, cites Lu Hsün's autobiographical work "Chao-hua hsi-shih," as providing a detailed description of the school, the San-wei shu-wu, in the chapter entitled "Ts'ung Po-ts'ao-yüan tao San-wei shu-wu"; see *Lu Hsün ch'üan-chi*, II, 384-90.

4. The grandfather's name was Chou Fu-ch'ing, his courtesy name Chieh-fu. A special study on him is Fang Chao-ying's "Kuan-yü Chou Fu-ch'ing ti shih-liao," *Ta-lu tsa-chih*, XV, no. 12 (December, 1957). Chou Tso-jen, in his essay "Wu-shih nien ch'ien ti Hang-chou fu-yü,"

describes what he remembers of his grandfather's life in prison from personal visits to the prison.

5. Chou's essay, "Wo ti tsa-hsüeh," ch. V; also, *Lu Hsün hsiao-shuo li ti jen-wu* (Shanghai, 1954), pp. 291-326. On the academy itself, see K. Biggerstaff, *The Early Modern Government Schools in China* (Ithaca, 1961), pp. 58-60.

6. Chou reports on his Peking interlude in 1905 in his essays "Pei-p'ing ti hao huai," "Pei-p'ing ti ch'un-t'ien," "Chiu jih-chi ch'ao," and also in his book *Lu Hsün hsiao-shuo li ti jen-wu,* p. 133.

7. On his student years in Japan, the following essays by Chou are particularly revealing: "Wo ti tsa-hsüeh," chs. V and VIII, "Liu-hsüeh ti hui-i," and "Wo hsüeh kuo-wen ti ching-yen." For general background information, see Roger F. Hackett, "Chinese students in Japan, 1900–1910," *Papers on China from the Regional Studies Seminar* (Harvard University, Cambridge, Mass., 1948), pp. 134-69; also, Brunnert and Hagelstrom, *Present Day Political Organization of China* (Shanghai, 1912).

8. The Japanese family name, a somewhat unusual one, is transcribed according to the pronunciation given in Gillis and Pai, *Japanese Surnames* (Peking, 1939), p. 65 (no. 3356); cf. Araki Ryōzō, *Nanori jiten* (Tokyo, 1959), p. 273.

9. On the question of family responsibility, see Olga Lang, *Chinese Family and Society* (New Haven, 1946), p. 164.

10. Lu Hsün, "Tzu-chuan," *Lu Hsün ch'üan-chi,* XX, 610.

11. Wang Ho-chao, "Hui-i Lu Hsün hsien-sheng" (Remembering Lu Hsün), *Pi-tuan,* IX (May 1, 1968), 19.

12. On inquiry, the Administrative Office of Rikkyo University, Tokyo, confirmed in 1967 that he had been registered as a student, but that there was no record of his graduation. *Gendai Chūgoku jimmei jiten* (Tokyo, 1966), p. 411, states that he "graduated from the Faculty of Literature of Rikkyo University."

13. See e.g., C. T. Hsia, *A History of Modern Chinese Fiction, 1917–1957* (New Haven, 1961), p. 31.

14. Ts'ai Yüan-p'ei (1867–1940), whose courtesy name was Chieh-min, was a native of Shaohsing, and the Chou and Ts'ai families had a history of friendly intercourse; see Chou's *Yao-wei-chi,* p. 58, and W. Schultz, *op. cit.,* p. 135, and the sources cited there. Ts'ai Yüan-p'ei obtained his *chin-shih* degree at the age of twenty-three and held office under the Ch'ing dynasty. He early aligned himself with the revolutionary forces in Shanghai, traveled to Europe and the United States, and became a political refugee in Japan. After the Revolution of 1911, he became the Republic's first minister of education; he was later appointed president of Peking National University and president of Academia Sinica. He is best remembered for

his liberal policies and his success in building National Peking University into a model institution of its kind. See Chiang Monlin, *Tides from the West* (New Haven, 1947), pp. 116-19. Chou Tso-jen wrote a eulogy of Ts'ai, "Chi Ts'ai Chieh-min hsien-sheng ti shih," *Yao-wei-chi,* pp. 58-67. See the chronological outline of his life in Sun Te-chung, ed., *Ts'ai Yüan-p'ei hsien-sheng i-wen lei-ch'ao* (Taipei, 1966); see also Tai Chin-hsieo, "The Life and Work of Ts'ai Yüan-p'ei," unpubl. diss. (Harvard, 1952).

15. See Chou's essays "Kuan-yü chin-tai san-wen" and "Chi Ts'ai Chieh-min hsien-sheng ti shih," where he gives an account of his early years in Peking.

16. In 1922, he became assistant professor of Chinese at Yenching University. He also occasionally lectured at Peking Women's Normal College; see, e.g., Fan Yin-nan, *Tang-tai Chung-kuo ming-jen lu* (Directory of Contemporary Chinese Personalities), (Preface, Shanghai, 1931), p. 130.

17. Ch'en (1880–1942) studied in Japan, where he first established contacts with Chinese revolutionaries. In 1915, he founded the *Hsin-ch'ing-nien* magazine in Shanghai. Later, he joined the faculty of Peking National University. Always an exponent of the radical Left, he became one of the founders of the Chinese Communist party but was expelled from the party in 1928 for "rightist opportunism." In 1932, he was arrested in Shanghai; he was imprisoned until 1937 and died near Chungking in 1942. O. Brière, "Une carrière orageuse, la vie de Tch'en Tou-Sieou, 1879–1942," *Bulletin de l'Université l'Aurore,* 3rd. ser., V (1944), 393-416. B. Schwartz, "Ch'en Tu-hsiu," *Journal of the History of Ideas,* XII, no. 1 (January 1951), 61-72; and by the same author, *Chinese Communism and the Rise of Mao* (Cambridge, Mass., 1952). H. L. Boorman, ed., *Biographical Dictionary of Republican China,* I (New York, 1967), 240-48.

18. (1891–1962), modern China's great liberal philosopher and academician; see O. Brière, "Un maître de la pensée en Chine, Hou Che," *Bulletin de l'Université l'Aurore,* 3rd Ser., V, no. 5 (1944), 871-93; VI, no. 1 (1945), 47-73; Irene Eber, "Hu Shih (1891–1962); a Sketch of his Life and his Role in the Intellectual and Political Dialogue of Modern China," unpubl. diss. (Claremont, 1966), with bibliography; van Boven, *L'Histoire de la Littérature Chinoise Moderne* (Tientsin, 1946), pp. 20-23, and for an earlier impression, *China Journal,* XXX, no. 1 (January, 1939), 58.

19. Ch'ien (1887–1938) studied in Tokyo under Chang T'ai-yen. On his return to China, he taught Chinese literature at Peking National University and other institutions in Peking. He was one of the early supporters of the *pai-hua* movement and a member of the *Hsin-ch'ing-nien* group of writers. "To exemplify his incredulous attitude

towards the past, he discarded in August, 1925, his original family name, taking instead the two characters *i-ku* 'Doubter of Antiquity'— the surname by which he is now known." Arthur W. Hummel, *The Autobiography of a Chinese Historian* (Leyden, 1931), p. 2, n. 2. Also see Hashikawa Tokio, *Chūgoku bunkakai jimbutsu sōkan* (General Survey of Chinese Literary Personalities) (Peking, 1940), pp. 88-90. For a short résumé of his relations with the Chou brothers, see Chao Ts'ung, *Chung-kuo wen-hsüeh-shih kang* (An Outline History of Chinese Literature) (Peking, 1940), pp. 88-90, and Lin Yin, "Ch'ien Hsüan-t'ung chuan lüeh" (A Short Biography of Ch'ien Hsüan-t'ung), *Ta-lu tsa-chih*, XXV, no. 12 (December, 1962), 13, and H. L. Boorman, ed., *op. cit.*, I (1967), 367-68.

20. Liu Fu (1891–1934), better known under his courtesy name Pan-nung, joined the faculty of Peking National University in 1917 and became a member of the *Hsin-ch'ing-nien* circle. After obtaining a doctorate in France, he returned to Peking University, where he associated himself with the Yü-ssu group as a writer of vernacular verse, essays, and criticism. A noted philologist, he died in 1934 as a consequence of a field trip to study local dialects. Chou Tso-jen wrote a eulogy on his friend; see *K'u-ch'a sui-pi*, pp. 157-63. Hashikawa Tokio, *op. cit.*, p. 685, and H. L. Boorman, ed., *op. cit.*, II (1968), 394-95.

21. "His most 'high-spirited' and most active years," is the judgment of K'ang Ssu-ch'ün in his article included in T'ao Ming-chih, ed., *Chou Tso-jen lun* (Shanghai, 1934), p. 4.

22. For details on these periodicals, see Chow Tse-tsung, *Research Guide to the May Fourth Movement* (Cambridge, Mass., 1963), pp. 29, 43, 109, 45, and 126-27, respectively. The *Guide* also mentions (p. 72) Chou Tso-jen as a contributor to the short-lived *Jen-tao yüeh-pao* and (p. 117) to the *Wen-hsüeh chou-pao*.

23. *Ibid.*, 102-3; also see Lou Tzu-k'uang and Chu Chieh-fan, *Wu-shih-nien lai ti Chung-kuo su wen-hsüeh* (Fifty Years of Chinese Popular Literature) (Taipei, 1963), pp. 115-18, for a chapter on the *Ko-yao chou-k'an*.

24. On Mushakoji Saneatsu, 1885–, see *Kindai Nihon bunka jiten* (Dictionary of Modern Japanese Literature) (Tokyo, 1963), pp. 384–85, and *Kindai bungaku kenkyu hikkei* (Vade Mecum of Modern Japanese Literature) (Tokyo, 1963), pp. 43-52. On his literary significance, see particularly Shinoda Tarō, *Kindai Nihon bungakushi* (History of Modern Japanese Literature) (Tokyo, 1932), p. 439, and I-chai, "Wu-che-hsiao-lu Shih-tu yin-hsiang-chi" (Impressions of Mushakoji Saneatsu), *I-wen tsa-chih*, I, no. 2 (August, 1943). In the September issue of the same periodical, a photo shows Mushakoji and Chou in front of the latter's studio in Peking. Mushakoji was

also a painter of note, and one of his pictures adorns the cover of Chou Tso-jen's *Yao-t'ang tsa-wen*, 1944 edition. For a more recent appreciation, see Ch'en Chi-ying's report on a visit to Mushakoji's Tokyo home in June, 1962, in *Chuan-chi wen-hsüeh*, I, no. 4 (September 1962), 31-34.

25. The *Atarashiki mura* is located at Hiuga, Miyazaki Prefecture, Kyushu. Mushakoji Saneatsu was one of the leading spirits in organizing the enterprise. Chou Tso-jen wrote several essays on his impressions of the New Village, e.g., in *Hsin-ch'ao*, II, no. 1 (October 1919), 69-90; "Hsin-ts'un ti ching-shen" in *Hsin-ch'ing-nien*, XII, no. 2 (January, 1920); "Fang Jih-pen hsin-ts'un chi" and "Hsin-ts'un ti li-hsiang yü shih-chi," both in Chou's *I-shu yü sheng-huo* (Peking, 1926); "Jih-pen ti hsin-ts'un" in *Hsin-ch'ing-nien*, VII, no. 3 (March 15, 1919), with additional remarks "Ta Yüan Chün-ch'ang chün" in the same periodical, VI, no. 6, p. 657. See also Chow Tse-tsung, *The May Fourth Movement* (Cambridge, Mass., 1960), pp. 190 and 425, ns. 54 and 55.

26. See especially C. T. Hsia, *op. cit.*, ch. III, "The Literary Research Society," and Ts'ao Chü-jen, *Wen-t'an wu-shih nien* (Fifty Years on the Literary Stage) (Hong Kong, 1955), I, 162-64; van Boven, *op. cit.*, pp. 39-60; William Ayres, "The Society for Literary Studies, 1921–1930," in *Papers on China from the Regional Studies Seminar* (Harvard University, Cambridge, Mass., 1948), VII, 40-42.

27. *Chung-kuo hsin-wen-hsüeh ta-hsi* (Anthology of Modern Chinese Literature) (Shanghai, 1935), X, 75–76, reproduces the manifesto; on its authorship, see Huo I-hsien, *Tsui-chin erh-shih nien Chung-kuo wen-hsüeh shih-kang* (Outline History of Chinese Literature During the Last Twenty Years) (Canton, 1936), p. 36, and Chou Tso-jen himself in "Wen-t'an chih-wai," *Li-ch'un i-ch'ien* (Shanghai, 1945), p. 162.

28. See Chow Tse-tsung, *Research Guide to the May Fourth Movement*, p. 124 (no. 590).

29. On the family quarrel, also see Chao Ts'ung, *Wu-ssu wen-t'an tien-ti* (Bits and Pieces on the May Fourth Literary Scene) (Hong Kong, 1964), chapter "Lu Hsün yü Chou Tso-jen" (Lu Hsün and Chou Tso-jen), pp. 91–93.

30. Lin Yutang (1895–   ), a native of Fukien Province, became particularly well known for his social satires and the publication of various widely circulating periodicals in the 1930's. His more popular books in English on Chinese thought and culture, among them *My Country and My People*, established his international reputation. From 1923 to 1926, he was professor in the English Department of Peking University. See H. L. Boorman, ed., *op. cit.*, II, 387-98; also J. Schyns,

1500 Modern Chinese Novels and Plays (Peking, 1948), p. 66, and van Boven, *op. cit.,* pp. 103-40. After extended periods of residence abroad, mostly in the United States, Lin took up permanent residence on Taiwan in 1966.

31. Sun Fu-yüan (1894–   ), a native of Shaohsing and once a student at Peking University, became a journalist and critic of influence, particularly as editor of the literary supplement of the Peking *Ch'en-pao* newspaper. He was a strong supporter of the *pai-hua* movement, one of the signators of the Manifesto of the Literary Research Society, and a frequent contributor to the *Yü-ssu* magazine. Particularly valuable are his translations of Tolstoy. He remained in Peking after 1949 and is listed as a member of various cultural organizations. See van Boven, *op. cit.,* pp. 55 and 94; *China Journal,* XXX, no. 3 (March 1939), 183; *Gendai Chūgoku jimmei jiten,* 1962 ed., p. 366, and 1966 ed., p. 559.

32. For a detailed account of the history of the *Yü-ssu* magazine, see Ch'uan Tao, "I Lu Hsün hsien-sheng ho Yü-ssu" (Remembering Mr. Lu Hsün and *Threads of Talk*) *Wen-i-pao,* XVI (August 30, 1956), 5-8. The name *Yü-ssu* was chosen by Ch'ien Hsüan-t'ung and Chou Tso-jen by opening a book at random and choosing suitable words they found on the opened page; see Lin Yutang in his article "Chi Chou shih hsiung-ti" (Memories of the Chou Brothers), *Chungyang jih-pao,* March 26, 1965; similarly, Ts'ao Chü-jen, *Wen-t'an wu-shih nien,* I, 160, quoting Lu Hsün. Hsieh Chou-k'ang translates the name as "Zeitschrift des gefälligen Wortes" in *Sinica,* VII, no. 1, p. 18, but W. Schultz, *op. cit.,* p. 31, uses the more appropriate term "Threads of Talk." Lin Yutang in the article mentioned above associates the name with *san-ssu,* scattered (random) threads.

33. This was the same government order that made Lu Hsün and Lin Yutang leave Peking; see H. L. Boorman, ed., *op. cit.,* II, 387, also Huo I-hsien, *op. cit.,* p. 38.

34. Matsueda Shigeo, *op. cit.,* p. 307, lines 3-4. Chou Tso-jen recounts the incident in his eulogy of Liu Pan-nung in *K'u-ch'a sui-pi,* pp. 160-62, and again quotes Liu Pan-nung's account of the incident in *Kuo-ch'ü ti kung-tso,* p. 64.

35. Her picture and a commemorative essay are contained in *Yü-t'ien ti shu* (Peking, 1925).

36. "Chou Tso-jen tzu-shu," in T'ao Ming-chih, ed., *Chou Tso-jen lun,* p. 1.

37. See e.g., H. S. Quigley, *China's Politics in Perspective* (Minneapolis, 1960), pp. 73-74, under the heading "Kuomintang Terrorism."

38. See, for instance, Chou's essay "Tao-ch'i Teng-ts'un" (Shimazaki

Tōson), *Yao-t'ang tsa-wen*, p. 111, lines 8-9; also, T'ao Ming-chih in his preface to *Chou Tso-jen lun*, p. 3.

39. G. E. Taylor, *Struggle for North China* (New York, 1940), p. 88. The estimate is even somewhat higher—about 2,000—in *U.S. Office of Education Bulletin 1945*, no. 3, "Education under Enemy Occupation," p. 12.

40. See the report by Ch'eng Chien-chien headed "Ti-jen jo-lan hsia ti Pei-ching ta-hsüeh" (Peking University under the Boots of the Enemy) in *Yü-chou-feng*, no. 74. Chiang Monlin, president of Peking University, also seems to have advised Chou Tso-jen to stay on, particularly in view of Chou's good relations with certain Japanese and the chance that he might be able to protect school property; see Liu Hsin-huang in *Ch'uang-tso*, I (May, 1961), 84-85, and Hung Yen-ch'iu, "Wo so jen-shih ti Chou Tso-jen" (The Chou Tso-jen I Knew), *Ch'un-wen-hsüeh*, II, no. 1 (July, 1967).

41. The letter dated London, August 4, 1938, is quoted in Ch'en Chih-fan, *Tsai ch'un-feng li* (Taipei, 1962), pp. 103-4.

42. The text of Chou's reply to Hu Shih, September 21, 1938, was communicated to the writer by Professor Liu Ts'un-yan.

43. *Pi-tuan*, no. 1 (January 1, 1968), 11-12.

44. See especially Matsueda Shigeo, *op. cit.*, 325-26. In the *Gendai Shina jimmei jiten* (Biographical Dictionary of Modern China) (Tokyo, 1939), p. 181, the assailant is described as a Communist. Others, like Sato Haruo, in *Shu Sakujin sensei no koto* (About Chou Tso-jen), ed. by Fang Chi-sheng (Tokyo, 1944), p. 49, describe him as a nationalist.

45. Liu Hsin-huang, "Kuan-yü Chou Tso-jen," *Ch'uang-tso*, no. 1 (August, 1961), p. 85.

46. Hung Yen-ch'iu, *op. cit.*, p. 72.

47. See Huang Shang, *Chin-fan chi-wai* (Shanghai, 1948), pp. 228 and 239. Chou repeats his accusation against the Japanese military in his letter to Hsü Hsü dated February 10, 1966; see *Pi-tuan*, no. 1 (January 1, 1968), 12.

48. G. E. Taylor, *op. cit.*, p. 89.

49. See Chou's own essay "Tao-ch'i T'eng-ts'un" (Shimazaki Tōson), *Yao-t'ang tsa-wen*, p. 112.

50. The Shanghai *Ta-kung-pao* reported his transfer to Nanking and some of the trial sessions in its issues of June 6, August 11, and September 21, 1946.

51. Ch'en Chih-fan, *op. cit.*, pp. 104 ff.

52. An account of this episode is contained in Lin Yutang, *The Gay Genius* (New York, 1947), pp. 193-94.

53. Both J. Schyns, *op. cit.*, p. 27, and C. T. Hsia, *op. cit.*, p. 322, state that the final sentence was for ten years, as does Hung Yen-ch'iu,

op. cit., p. 72, line 10. These statements are confirmed by Chu Tzu-chia, pseudonym of the lawyer Chin Hsiung-pai, who was sentenced to a little over two years at about the same time, in his *Wang cheng-ch'uan ti k'ai-ch'ang yü shou-ch'ang* (The Wang Ching-wei Regime, from Overture to Curtain Drop) (Hong Kong, 1961), IV, 91-92.

54. Chin Tien-jung, "Chou Tso-jen Kuan I-hsing t'ao ssu-hsing chi" (How Chou Tso-jen and Kuan I-hsing Escaped the Death Penalty), *Ch'un-ch'iu tsa-chih,* no. 197 (September 15, 1965), 5-7. On the other hand, the Shanghai *Ta-kung-pao,* although not mentioning Chou by name, reports on February 8, 1949, the release of all prisoners with ten years or shorter prison terms, "many of them traitors from the time of the enemy occupation." This would also agree approximately with the time that Chou resumed his diary (April 1, 1949), which he said he did not keep in prison; see *Pi-tuan,* no. 9 (May 1, 1968), p. 5.

55. For details of Chou's request and preparations by his friends to have him come to Taiwan; see Hung Yen-ch'iu, *op. cit.,* p. 72, lines 15-19.

56. *T'oung Pao,* XLIX, nos. 4-5 (1961), 357-404.

57. Ts'ao Chü-jen, a leftist Hong Kong journalist, visited Chou in 1957 and obtained from him material for publication in Hong Kong; see Chou's own preface to his *Chih-t'ang i-yu wen-pien.* Ts'ao Chü-jen mentions visits to Chou in his *Pei-hsing erh-yü* (Hong Kong, 1960), pp. 149 and 153, and *Pei-hsing san-yü* (Hong Kong, 1963), pp. 48, 49, 51, and 163.

Chu P'u, courtesy name Hsing-chai, a Hong Kong publisher, reports in the Hong Kong magazine *Ta-hua* (Cathay Review), no. 28 (April 30, 1967), 2, that he visited Chou Tso-jen in Peking in 1957, 1960, and 1963.

Professor Ando Kōsei of Waseda University, Tokyo, who considers himself a student of Chou Tso-jen, published a comprehensive report on his visit to Chou in the article "Ku'usai hōmonki" (Visit to the "Bitter Rain Studio"), *Daian,* no. 98 (January, 1964), 1-4.

58. Chu P'u, *op. cit.,* p. 2.

In May 1970, the *Chih-t'ang hui-hsiang lu* (Memoirs of Chou Tso-jen), 727 pp., were published in Hong Kong. These autobiographical essays were purportedly written by Chou in the early 1960's and entrusted to Ts'ao Chü-jen for publication abroad. Despite a few hitherto unknown details of his life, the work is generally disappointing for a paucity of new factual information and repetitiousness throughout. He seems to have tried, obviously without much enthusiasm, to exploit further an already well-worked subject, apparently forced to do so by the necessity to support himself in his old age.

Chapter Two

1. The definition of the essay found in Webster's *Dictionary* is: "analytical or interpretative in nature, dealing with its subject from a more or less limited, or personal standpoint and permitting a considerable freedom of style and method. . . ." Other useful definitions are contained in B. C. Williams, *A Book of Essays* (Boston, 1931), pp. 243-61; Hugh Walker, *The English Essay and Essayists* (London, 1915); Introduction, pp. 1-4; R. A. Witham, *Essays of Today* (Boston, 1931), p. xx; Kurt Wais, "Antwort auf eine Umfrage über den Essay," *An den Grenzen der Nationalliteraturen* (Berlin, 1958), pp. 338-40.

2. A comprehensive and still valid study of the origin of the European essay is contained in the "Remarks on Essay Writing," *North American Review,* (April, 1822), 319-50. This article points to precursors of the European essay in classical times, e.g., the *Noctes atticae* by Gellius (ca. A.D. 130). Similarly, J. A. K. Thomson, *The Classical Background of English Literature* (London, 1948) and *Classical Influences on English Prose* (London, 1956), referring particularly to Seneca and Plutarch as "creating the climate of mind, favorable to free speculation on moral and personal problems, which made possible the *essais* of Montaigne and the essays of Bacon"; see *Classical Influences on English Prose,* p. 157.

3. Of a different opinion: Chung Ching-wen, "Shih t'an hsiao-p'in wen" (A tentative discourse on the essay) in Ah-ying, ed., *Hsien-tai shih-liu chia hsiao-p'in* (Sixteen Modern Essayists) (Shanghai, 1935), p. 115, where Chuang-tzu's short stories are indeed considered essays. For two recent English renderings of Chuang-tzu, see Thomas Merton, *The Way of Chuang Tzu* (New York, 1965), and Burton Watson, *Chuang Tzu, Basic Writings* (New York, 1964), both with copious bibliographies.

4. "The *Shih-shuo hsin-yü* is a collection of anecdotes about officials, savants, and eccentrics who lived in the period from the last years of the Han to the close of the Chin dynasty—from the late second century to the early fifth—brought together by Liu I-ch'ing (403–444), a nephew of the first Sung emperor," Yoshikawa Kojiro, "The *Shih-shuo hsin-yü and* Six Dynasties Prose Style," trans. by Glen W. Baxter, in *Harvard Journal of Asiatic Studies,* XVIII (1955), 124-44. See also Chen Shou-yi, *Chinese Literature* (New York, 1961), p. 274.

5. On the Seven Masters of the Chien-an period, see Cheng Chen-to, *Ch'a-t'u-pen Chung-kuo wen-hsüeh shih* (Peking, 1958), pp. 137-41.

6. See especially the interpretations by Kuo Shao-yü in his *Chung-kuo wen-hsüeh p'i-p'ing shih* (Peking, 1961), pp. 37-39.

7. Cheng Chen-to, *op. cit.,* p. 235.

8. Cheng Chen-to, *op. cit.*, pp. 233-58; also see E. D. Edwards, "A Classified Guide to the Thirteen Classes of Chinese Prose," *Bulletin of the School of Oriental and African Studies*, XII (1948), 770-88; Li Su-po, *Hsiao-p'in-wen yen-chiu* (A Study of the Essay) (Shanghai, 1932), pp. 28-32, and Shih Wei, ed., *Hsiao-p'in-wen chiang hua* (Discussions of the Essay) (Shanghai, 1935) with a comprehensive history of the Chinese essay, pp. 45-49.

9. A gifted and well-educated man who rose to high office. Among other offices, he was *nei-shih* (censor) at Kuei-chi, Chou Tso-jen's native place, but he resigned at the age of thirty-five to live as a recluse, espousing the Taoist naturalism of his time. His fame is due to the natural beauty of his style, as well as to his calligraphy; his writings are valued as examples of graphic art. See H. A. Giles, *A Chinese Biographical Dictionary*, p. 821. Wang's "Orchard Pavillion Preface" is translated in Lin Yutang, *Importance of Understanding* (Cleveland, 1960), p. 98, and again by J. D. Frodsham, *Asia Major*, VIII (1960/61), 90-91, with copious footnotes. Two modern monographs on Wang Hsi-chih are: Chu Chieh-ch'in, *Wang Hsi-chih p'ing-chuan* (Changsha, 1940), and Shen Tzu-shan, *Wang Hsi-chih yen-chiu* (Shanghai, 1948). How well Wang Hsi-chih's art agrees with our modern understanding of essay writing is revealed in the following description by Cheng Chen-to, *op. cit.*, p. 237: "The memoranda and sundry messages that he wrote, he would dash off at will and yet achieve naturalness and the highest effectiveness. His topics were trifling family affairs, dealings with relations and friends, presentations of gifts, kind words of consolation, and replies to enquiries. Although frequently only a few lines, they are serene and stirring, filled with sentiment and meaning that a thousand sheets seem unable to describe fully."

10. T'ao Ch'ien, better known by his sobriquet Yüan-ming, typifies the Chinese poet-recluse. He retired early in life from the pressures and frequent indignities of officialdom to live as a poor farmer. See William Acker, *T'ao the Hermit* (London, 1952); Lilly Chang and M. Sinclair, *The Poems of T'ao Ch'ien* (Honolulu, 1953); and Li Chen-tung, "T'ao Yüan-ming tso-p'in hsi nien," *Ta-lu tsa-chih*, II (1951), 11-15.

11. The apt English translation "literary notebook" was coined by Lin Yutang, *op. cit.*, p. 14.

12. The *shuo* as a literary genre is already mentioned by Liu Hsieh, A.D. 465–522, in his *Wen-hsin tiao-lung*, China's first comprehensive work on literary criticism, ch. XVIII, together with another similar genre called the *lun*, which E. D. Edwards, *op. cit.*, p. 771, translates as "essay or disquisition." See also Vincent Shih, *The Literary Mind and the Carving of Dragons* (New York, 1959), a complete transla-

tion of the Wen-hsin tiao-lung, where (p. 101) *shuo* is translated as "discussion."

13. The *Wen-hsüan* anthology was compiled by Hsiao T'ung (501–531). An almost complete German translation is E. von Zach's *Die Chinesische Anthologie,* Harvard-Yenching Institute Studies no. 18 (Cambridge, Mass., 1958). See also J. R. Hightower, "The Wen-hsüan and Genre Theory," *Harvard Journal of Asiatic Studies,* XX (1957), 512-33.

14. On Han Yü and Liu Tsung-yüan in this particular context, see Shih Wei, *op. cit.,* p. 46, and Chou Tsu-mu and Ch'en Chin-chung, *Chung-kuo wen-hsüeh shih* (A History of Chinese Literature) (Amoy, 1965), pp. 122-24.

15. See especially Chen Shou-yi, *op. cit.,* pp. 350-90: "Sung Literature."

16. Günther Debon, *Ts'ang-lang's Gespräche über die Dichtung* (Wiesbaden, 1962), p. 5.

17. Lu Ch'ien, *Pa-ku-wen hsiao-shih* (A Short History of *Pa-ku* Prose) (Shanghai, 1937). Chou Tso-jen wrote an essay "Lun pa-ku-wen" (On *Pa-ku* Prose), in which he urged that training in this style be kept on the school curricula because of its significance in Chinese literary history.

18. On these two literary schools, see Chen Shou-yi, *op. cit.,* pp. 514-15; Cheng Chen-to, *op. cit.,* pp. 938-58.

19. Chou Tso-jen, *Chung-kuo hsin-wen-hsüeh ti yüan-liu* (The Sources of China's Modern Literature) (Peking, 1932), p. 43. Other opinions on this point: Chen Shou-yi, *op. cit.,* pp. 513-15; Ts'ao Chü-jen, *Wen-t'an wu-shih nien* (Hong Kong, 1955), *cheng chi,* p. 152; Chao Ts'ung, *Chung-kuo wen-hsüeh shih-kang* (Hong Kong, 1959), p. 135; Lin Yutang, "Lun wen," *Lin Yü-t'ang wen-hsüan* (Taipei, 1962), pp. 31-32; Feng Ming-chih, *Chung-kuo wen-hsüeh shih-hua* (Hong Kong, 1962), p. 441.

20. T'ang Ch'en in a review article in *Hsin-yüeh,* IV, no. 3 (1932), and Shih Wei, *op. cit.,* p. 80, express the same opinion.

Chapter Three

1. For general information on the Chinese classics, the *Ssu-shu* and *Wu-ching,* see A. Wylie, *Notes on Chinese Literature* (Shanghai, 1867), pp. 1-8; also S. Couling, "Classics," Encyclopaedia Sinica (Shanghai, 1917), p. 122. On their position in the prereform curriculum, see W. A. P. Martin, *The Chinese, Their Education, Philosophy, and Letters* (New York, 1881), pp. 57-82, and especially p. 64: "Stages of Study."

2. The full title of the book is *Ch'i-ch'iao pa-fen t'u*, a kind of pictorial encyclopedia, subdivided into sixteen topical sections, such as stars, human affairs, music, houses, etc. It is listed in Hu Wen-k'ai, *Li-tai fu-nü chu-tso k'ao* (Works by Women Authors throughout Past Generations) (Shanghai, 1957), pp. 572-73, where the authoress is given as Ch'ien Yün-chi and the date of publication as 1875.

3. From Chou's essay "Ch'i-ch'iao t'u," in *Shu-fang i-chiao*, pp. 14-15.

4. *Ching-hua-yüan* by Li Ju-chen (1763–1830) is in the nature of *Gulliver's Travels*. It is one of the several novels of political and social criticism at the end of the Ch'ing dynasty. For a synopsis of the book see Chen Shou-yi, *op. cit.*, pp. 590-93. Six partial translations into English, one by Lin Yutang, are listed by Martha Davidson, *A List of Published Translations from Chinese into English, French, and German. Part I: Literature, excl. Poetry* (Ann Arbor, Mich., 1952), p. 3. The Ta-t'ung Press edition of the book (1923) contains a lengthy scholarly preface by Hu Shih, who also wrote several articles in English on the significance of this novel, particularly on the women's question; see J. Lust, *Index Sinicus* (Cambridge, England, 1964), nos. 12152-12154.

5. All nine titles are well-known popular novels. They are described in Chen Shou-yi, *op. cit.*, Ou Itai, *Le Roman Chinois* (Paris, 1933); C. T. Hsia, *The Classic Chinese Novel*, (New York, 1968); Lu Hsün, *A Brief History of Chinese Fiction*, trans. by Yang Hsien-yi and Gladys Yang (Peking, 1959). On the *Feng-shen-chuan*, see Liu Tsun-yan, *The Authorship of the Feng-shen yen-i*, in *Buddhist and Taoist Influences on Chinese Novels*, I (Wiesbaden, 1962).

6. "Hsiao shuo," *Shu-fang-i-chiao*, p. 12.

7. "Hsiao-shuo ti hui-i," *Chih-t'ang i-yu wen-pien*, p. 9. The same idea is also expressed in "Wo ti tsa-hsüeh," *K'u-k'ou kan-k'ou*, p. 57.

8. Membership in the *Han-lin-yüan* (Imperial Academy) was the highest literary honor a scholar could aspire to under the Imperial regime; see W. A. P. Martin, *op. cit.*, pp. 1-38: "The Hanlin Yüan, or Imperial Academy." On the history of the institution, see F. A. Bishop, *Forêt des Pinceaux* (Paris, 1963). Chou's grandfather became a *Han-lin* member in 1875; see Fang Chao-ying, "Kuan-yü Chou Fu-ch'ing ti shih-liao," *Ta-lu tsa-chih*, XV, no. 12 (December, 1957), 377.

9. "Ching-hua-yüan," *Tzu-chi ti yüan-ti*, 1935 ed., p. 147. Cf. "Wo hsüeh kuo-wen ti ching-yen," *Chou Tso-jen wen-hsüan*, pp. 58-59. In *Yeh-tu-ch'ao*, p. 111, there is the passage: "just like grandfather would say, this [the mythological adventure novel *Hsi-yu-chi*] is apt to develop children's minds."

10. In the case of his elder brother Lu Hsün, we have his explicit

statement: "My mother asked me to find a tuition-free school," "Tzu-chuan" (autobiography), *Lu Hsün ch'üan chi*, XX, 609.

11. Lin Shu (1852–1924) is described in A. W. Hummel, ed., *Eminent Chinese in the Ch'ing Period* (Washington, 1943–44), p. 306, as "poet and painter, who rendered into Chinese, in whole or in part, with the help of translators, 156 titles of Western fiction, including such classics as *David Copperfield, Oliver Twist, Ivanhoe, Gulliver's Travels, . . .*" Chou Tso-jen expressed his appreciation of Lin Shu in his essay "Lin Ch'in-nan yü Lo Chen-yü," *Yü-ssu*, no. 2 (Dec. 1, 1924), 5: "Frankly, it was only because of Lin's translations that most of us came to know that the Western countries had novels, and some interest was thus aroused in foreign literature. Moreover, I personally very much emulated his translations." For a listing of Lin Shu's translations, see Ma T'ai-lai, "Lin Ch'in-nan so i hsiao-shuo shu-mu," *Ch'u-pan yüeh-k'an*, II, no. 12 (May 1, 1967), 73-79.

12. Yen Fu (1853–1921), the other great translator of this period, had the advantage over Lin Shu of knowing English—he had graduated from the Greenwich Naval College—and he concentrated his efforts on Western scientific and sociological works. Best known is his translation of T. H. Huxley's *Evolution and Ethics* under the translated title *T'ien-yen-lun* B. I. Schwartz, *In Search of Wealth and Power, Yen Fu and the West* (Cambridge, Mass., 1964).

13. *Yü t'ien ti shu*, pp. 48-49.

14. The Naval Academy had stopped manufacturing torpedoes, which may explain the reference to an "empty torpedo hall"; see J. L. Rawlinson, *China's Struggle for Naval Development, 1839–1895* (Cambridge, Mass., 1967), p. 156.

15. "Hsüeh-hsiao sheng-huo ti-i-yeh," *Yü-t'ien ti shu*, pp. 49-50. Chou Tso-jen's novel has been reprinted in Ah-ying, ed., *Wan-Ch'ing wen-hsüeh ts'ung-ch'ao* (Peking, 1961), section "Hsiao-shuo ssu-chuan," pp. 497 ff. under the misspelled pseudonym P'ing-yün, but without revealing the identity of the author—which no doubt must have been known to Ah-ying—in the preface, which treats of the motivation and alleged social purport of the novel.

16. Confucius, *Lun-yü*, II, 17, in Legge's translation.

17. *Yao-wei-chi*, preface, and p. 64; also in "Yin-shu-chih," *Shu-fang i chiao*, p. 96, and "Wo ti tsa-hsüeh," *K'u-k'ou kan-k'ou*, p. 61.

18. T. Prokora, "Necessity of a More Thorough Study of Philosopher Wang Ch'ung and His Predecessors," *Archiv Orientalni*, XXX (1962), 232, and "The Works of Wang Ch'ung," *ibid.*, XXXVI (1968), 122-33. A translation by Alfred Forke (Leipzig, 1906) was republished in 1962. For supplemental notes, see Donald Leslie, "Contributions to a New Translation of the Lun-heng," *T'oung Pao*, XLIV, livre 2-3 (1956), 100-149. Admiration for Wang Ch'ung's "modern"

way of thinking is expressed by Hu Shih, "Scientific Spirit and Method in China," *Philosophy and Culture East and West* (1962), 205-8. Similarly, Feng Yu-lan, *A History of Chinese Philosophy,* II (Princeton, 1953), pp. 150-67; also G. Willoughby-Meade, "A Chinese Sceptic," in *Chinese Ghouls and Goblins* (London, 1928), pp. 334-54. A more recent summation is Chiang Tsu-i, *Wang Ch'ung ti wen-hsüeh li-lun* (Wang Ch'ung's Literary Theories) (Peking, 1962).

19. K. C. Hsiao, "Li Chih; an Iconoclast of the 16th Century," *Tien Hsia Monthly,* VI (1938), 317-41; Otto Franke, "Li Tschi; ein Beitrag zur Geschichte der chinesischen Geisteskämpfe im 16. Jahrhundert," *Mitteilungen der Preussischen Akademie der Wissenschaften,* 1937, 1-62; also Jung Chao-tsu, *Li Cho-wu p'ing-chuan* (Critique and Biography of Li Chih) (Shanghai, 1937). On Wang Yang-ming, see Henke, *The Philosophy of Wang Yang-ming* (London, 1916).

20. A. W. Hummel, ed., *op. cit.,* pp. 936-37, and sources quoted there. An English treatise on Yü is Lin Yutang's article "Feminist Thought in Ancient China," *T'ien Hsia Monthly,* I, no. 2 (September, 1935), 127-50.

21. Spencer and Huxley were made popular in China through the translations of Yen Fu; on this subject, see B. I. Schwartz, *op. cit.,* pp. 98-112: "Evolution and Ethics." Nietzsche's *Zarathustra* had been translated by Kuo Mo-jo; see *Chung-kuo hsin-wen-hsüeh ta-hsi,* X, 374. One of his books Chou Tso-jen prefaced with a quotation from Nietzsche and chose for its title the words *Tien-ti* (Drops) from the quotation. In a later republication (1928) however he omitted the Nietzschean quote and changed the title to *K'ung-ta-ku* (Empty Drums), the title of a Tolstoy short story.

22. Havelock Ellis (1859–1939), an English medical scientist, writer, and social reformer, particularly interested in social, individual, and sex psychology; see I. Goldberg, *Havelock Ellis, a Biographical and Critical Survey* (New York, 1926); A. Colder-Marshall, *The Sage of Sex; a Life of Havelock Ellis* (New York, 1959); and J. S. Collis, *Havelock Ellis, Artist of Life* (New York, 1959).

23. See, for instance, the chapter "Sang-hsia ts'ung-t'an," in *Shu-fang i-chiao.* It is also significant that Chou Tso-jen was asked to write a postscript when the *Yüeh-yen,* a book on the customs and folklore of the Shaohsing area, compiled by Fan Yin and first published in 1882, was republished in 1932 by the Lai Hsün Ko publishing house in Peking.

24. Preface to *T'an-lung-chi,* p. 7.

25. The definition of *sophrosyne* given in the text is from the *Century Dictionary.* The translation of the Chinese *chung-yung* by *sophrosyne* is suggested by Chou is his essays "Shang-hai ch'i," *T'an-lung-chi,* p. 159, and "Kua-tou-chi t'i-chi," *Chou Tso-jen tai-piao-tso*

hsüan (Collection of Representative Works of Chou Tso-jen), Chang Chün, ed. (n.p., 1938), p. 225. In "Sheng-shu yü Chung-kuo wen-hsüeh," *Hsiao-shuo yüeh-pao,* XII, no. 1 (January 10, 1921), 4, Chou equates it with *chung-ho* ("middle/temperate" and "harmonious").

26. Kurt Wais, "Antwort auf eine Umfrage über den Essay," p. 338; Lin Yutang expressed the same idea with the Chinese phrase *i tzu-wo wei chung-hsin* (with one's very self as center), see the Preface to *Lin Yü-t'ang wen-hsüeh hsüan* (Taipei, 1962).

Chapter Four

1. Shih Chih-ts'un, "Tsa-wen ti wen-i chia-chih," *Wen-fan hsiao-p'in,* V (June, 1935), p. 38.

2. To argue the philosophy of art here would lead us too far afield. I follow Lascelles Abercrombie, *An Essay Towards the Theory of Art* (London, 1922), p. 74: "The essential thing involved in artistic expression is that the expression must also be communication." Also Kurt Schilling, *Die Kunst* (Meisenheim/Glan, 1961), p. 103: "Urteile über Kunst grundsätzlich nicht Beurteilungen eines Gegenstandes sein können, sondern nur Reflexionsurteile über den Urteilenden selbst in Hinblick auf den Gegenstand."

3. Concerning this question, see C. T. Hsia, *A History of Modern Chinese Fiction, 1917–1957* (New Haven, 1961), pp. 5-13.

4. Hu Shih, "Wu-shih nien lai Chung-kuo chih wen-hsüeh" (Fifty Years of Chinese Literature), *Hu Shih wen-ts'un, erh-chi* (Shanghai, 1922), p. 91.

5. Hu Shih, *Pai-hua wen-hsüeh shih* (Shanghai: 1929; republished Taipei 1957); also see J. L. Bishop, *The Colloquial Short Story in China* (Cambridge, Mass., 1956).

6. *Chung-kuo hsin-wen-hsüeh ti yüan-liu,* 111-12. The adoption of the new literary *pai-hua* was not without its intermediary phases; see, for instance, J. R. Levenson, *Liang Ch'i-ch'ao and the Mind of Modern China* (Cambridge, Mass., 1959), p. 23. On Liang's style, which was a compromise between *wen-yen* and the colloquial, later also employed by Sun Yat-sen, see C. T. Hsia, *op. cit.,* p. 6.

7. On opposition to the *pai-hua* movement, see C. T. Hsia, *ibid.,* p. 13.

8. These expressions occur in *Tzu-chi ti yüan-ti,* p. 154, "Huai Tung-ching chih erh," and "Kuan-yü chia hsün," respectively. Lin Yutang ridiculed these concerns for the enrichment of the Chinese language by the Chou brothers and their friends; see his article "Chi Chou-shih hsiung-ti," *Chung-yang jih-pao,* March 26, 1965.

9. Chou Tso-jen, "Hsin ming-tz'u," in "Kuo-ts'ui yü Ou-hua," *Tzu-*

chi ti yüan-ti, p. 113, Chou warns of excesses, such as the adoption of plural endings in imitation of foreign languages.

10. Chou Tso-jen, "Shih-chieh-yü tu-pen," *Tzu-chi ti yüan-ti,* pp. 155-58; "Wo ti tsa-hsüeh," ch. XVIII; and "Kuo-yü kai-tsao ti i-tien," *I-shu yü sheng-huo,* p. 102.

11. In his foreword to "Kai ko," *Hsin-ch'ing-nien,* V, no. 2 (August 15, 1918), he states that this new Chinese character with the *nü* radical was invented by Liu Pan-nung.

12. Hu Shih, "Chien-she ti wen-hsüeh ko-ming lun," *Hu Shih wen-ts'un,* I (Shanghai, 1921), p. 77; Chou Tso-jen, *Chung-kuo hsin-wen-hsüeh ti yüan-liu,* pp. 103-4, and "Kuo-yü wen-hsüeh t'an," *I-shu yü sheng-huo,* p. 126. Concurring with Chou's views was Chu Ching-nung, who is quoted in van Boven, *op. cit.,* p. 27.

13. Chou Tso-jen's early translations, as those of Lu Hsün, were done in *wen-yen;* examples are *Yü-wai hsiao-shuo chi, T'an-hua, Hung-hsing i-shih, Hsiung-nu ch'i-shih lu.*

14. Han Shih-heng in T'ao Ming-chih, ed., *Chou Tso-jen lun* (Shanghai, 1934), p. 146.

15. "Wo hsüeh kuo-wen ti ching-yen," *Chou Tso-jen wen-hsüan,* p. 56; also, "Wo ti tsa-hsüeh," ch. II.

16. In the essay "Chiu-shu hui-hsiang chi" (Memories of Old Books), Chou mentions that as a fourteen-year-old boy he read the *Sung-yin man-lu* by Wang T'ao (1828-97) and the *Yüeh-wei-ts'ao-t'ang pi-chi* by Chi Yün (1724-1805); both books are described in A. W. Hummel, ed., *op. cit.,* pp. 838-39 and p. 123, respectively.

17. Ts'ai Yüan-p'ei, president of Peking University, in his reply to Lin Shu in the *pai-hua* controversy, testified to Chou Tso-jen's great erudition in traditional Chinese literature. The letter, dated December, 1918, is quoted by Wang Shih-tung in *Hsin-wen-hsüeh p'ing-lun* (Shanghai, 1920), p. 11.

18. Fei Ming (pseudonym of Feng Wen-ping) in his article in *Chou Tso-jen lun,* p. 25.

19. H. N. Fairchild, *An Approach to Literature* (New York, 1929), p. 37. It is the idea expressed in the famous dictum "Le style est l'homme même"; see G. L. L. Buffon (1707-88) in his "Discours prononcés à l'Academie Française" (August 25, 1753), *Oeuvres Complètes de Buffon* (Paris, 1824), I, p. CLX.

20. An appreciation of Wang Ch'ung's style is, for instance, also contained in Hu Shih, *Pai-hua wen-hsüeh shih,* pp. 51-54.

21. Chang Hsi-shen in the Preface to *Chou Tso-jen san-wen ch'ao* (Shanghai, 1933), p. 1.

22. The poem "Hsiao-ho" was first published in Hsin-ch'ing-nien, VI, no. 2 (February 15, 1919). Later this and several other *pai-hua* poems were published in the collection *Hsüeh-chao* (Snowy Morning)

(Shanghai, 1930), and in *Kuo-ch'ü ti sheng-ming* (Past Life) (Shanghai, 1930). "Hsiao-ho" and three other poems in English translation are to be found in H. Acton and Chen Shih-hsiang, *Modern Chinese Poetry* (London, 1936), pp. 53-54. All early *pai-hua* poems are to some extent in the nature of linguistic experiments; cf. Hu Shih's pioneering *Ch'ang-shih-chi* (Collection of Experiments) (Shanghai, 1920).

23. See ch. II, n. 12.

24. The *Shih-p'in*, the full title of which is *Erh-shih-ssu shih-p'in* (Twenty-four Poetic Qualities), is "a critical evaluation of poetry composed in Taoist spirit and mystic language," as aptly described by Günther Debon, *op. cit.*, p. 4. A complete translation of the *Shih-p'in* by Yang Hsien-i and Gladys Yang is to be found in *Chinese Literature*, 1963, no. 7.

25. Even so highly qualified a translator as Lin Yutang admits that in this field one will "run across phrases that are extremely difficult to render into English"; see "A Chinese Critical Vocabulary" in his *The Importance of Living* (New York, 1937), pp. 430-31.

26. Lin Yutang, *ibid.*, pp. 442-43, defines these terms as follows:
> *ch'ing:* clear, lucid, pure, clean, not profuse, not obstructed, not burdened with details, like an autumn landscape.
>
> *tan:* mild, pale in color, as of a misty lake. Probably the quality in a painting or writing that gives the greatest pleasure to a man of mature taste is *ch'ing-tan* (lucid and mild), p'ing-tan ("even and mild," the natural aroma of simple writing).

27. K'ang Ssu-ch'ün in his article in *Chou Tso-jen lun*, p. 10.

28. See Nihon Gakujutsu Shinkokai, *Haikai and Haiku* (Tokyo, 1958), p. 142.

29. See I. Goldberg, *Havelock Ellis*, p. 88.

30. See his essay "Tse-hsieh chi-hsü," also quoted in *Cho Tso-jen lun*, p. 5.

31. Lin Yutang, *Importance of Understanding*, p. 16.

32. In the first preface to *Yü-t'ien ti shu*, p. 6.

33. *Ibid.*, p. 1.

34. Preface to *K'an-yün-chi*, p. 2.

35. To be found, for instance, in the Wang Wei anthology *Wang yu-ch'eng chi chien-chu* (Peking, 1961), p. 35.

36. The title quotes the last symbolic words of Voltaire's *Candide:* "Il faut cultiver notre jardin."

37. *Tzu-chi ti yüan-ti*, 1935 ed., p. 175.

38. "Ho-ch'a," *Yü-t'ien ti shu*, p. 73.

39. A returned student from Japan, Yü's first novel, *Ch'en-lun*, was

published in 1921. For a detailed account of his life and significance, see C. T. Hsia, *op. cit.,* pp. 102-11.

40. *Ibid.,* p. 103.

41. Edward Carpenter (1844–1929), an English writer and social reformer, who dealt largely with sex questions (*Love's Coming of Age,* 1896) in a style that made his writings literature; see T. H. Bell, *Edward Carpenter: the English Tolstoi* (Los Angeles, 1932).

42. First published in the *Hsiao-shuo yüeh-pao,* XIII, no. 2 (February 1, 1922).

43. In the foreword to his poem "Hsiao-ho" (see note 22 above) as published in the *Hsin-ch'ing-nien,* VI, no. 2 (February 15, 1919).

44. The translations appear as *Yu-tzu* and *Ch'uang* in *Hsiao-shuo yüeh-pao,* XIII, no. 3 (March 10, 1922) and no. 6 (June 10, 1922).

45. In *Yü-ssu,* no. 10 (January 19, 1925), 1.

46. See Chu Chao-lo, "T'an hsiao-p'in-wen," *I-wen tsa-chih,* I, no. 2 (August, 1943).

47. Lao She is the pseudonym of Shu Ch'ing-ch'un (1898–1966), about whom see particularly C. T. Hsia, *op. cit.,* pp. 165-88.

48. In a letter addressed to Ch'uan Tao (pseudonym of Chang Ting-ch'ien) published in *Yü-ssu,* no. 17 (March, 1925), 8. This story is also found in an anthology of comic stories called *Ch'uan-chia-pao* (Thesaurus of Stories Handed Down in the Family) and compiled by Shih Ch'eng-chin of the early Ch'ing era. It is again mentioned in Chou Tso-jen's *K'u-ch'a sui-pi,* p. 335.

49. Chung-shu-chün (pseudonym of Ch'ien Chung-shu) in his article in *Chou Tso-jen lun,* p. 154.

50. See Chou's essay "Hua-chi ssu pu tuo" (A Seeming Lack of Humor), *Yü-ssu,* no. 8 (January 5, 1925), 8.

51. See his Introduction to *K'uang-yen shih fan* (Ten Kyogen Plays) (Peking, 1926), a book that contains Chou's translation of ten representative *kyogen* plays.

52. Chou Tso-jen translated two of Jonathan Swift's essays, namely "Direction of Servants" as "Pi-p'u hsü chih" and "A Modest Proposal" as "Yü-ying ch'u-i"; both translations are reproduced in *Chung-kuo hsin-wen-hsüeh ta-hsi,* X, 362.

53. Cf. his essay "Chung-kuo ti hua-chi wen-hsüeh" (China's Humorous Literature), *Yü-chou-feng,* no. 23.

Chapter Five

1. "Liang-ko kuei ti wen-chang" in *Kuo-ch'ü ti kung-tso,* p. 76.

2. At least for the term "hsien" we can adduce the authority of Lin Yutang, who gives the following definition in *The Importance of Living,* p. 443: "Leisure, leisurely. A very much used word. Thus

one's hands and mind can both be leisurely, or the hands may be leisurely while the mind is busy, or the mind may be leisurely while the hands are busy."

3. See p. 18.

4. "Pei-p'ing ti hao-huai, " *Yü-chou-feng*, no. 19 (June 16, 1936). A very short reference to the coarseness of the plays that he had witnesed in Peking in 1905 is contained in an earlier essay "Chung-kuo hsi-ch'ü ti san t'iao lu," *I-shu yü sheng-huo*, p. 90.

5. *Lu Hsün hsiao-shuo li ti jen-wu*, pp. 133-34.

6. Chou Tso-jen was but one of many reformers who condemned the form, content, and technique of the traditional drama. *Chung-kuo hsin-wen-hsüeh ta-hsi*, II, contains eleven representative critical essays, among them being Chou's "Lun Chung-kuo chiu-hsi chih ying fei" (On the Need to Abolish Old Chinese Stage Plays), which was first published in *Hsin ch'ing-nien*, V, no. 5 (November 1918). On this question, see also Chao Ts'ung, *Wu-ssu wen-t'an tien-ti*, pp. 11-14; A. C. Scott, *Literature and the Arts in 20th Century China* (Garden City, 1963), pp. 35-52.

7. *Lu Hsün hsiao-shuo li ti jen-wu*, p. 134.

8. "Ch'in Jih p'ai," *T'an-hu-chi*, p. 19.

9. "Jih-pen chih tsai jen-shih," *Yao-wei-chi*, p. 230.

10. *Ibid.*, p. 231. Similar remarks about Japan having become a second home are also attributed, for instance, to Chou's illustrious compatriot Liang Ch'i-ch'ao; see J. R. Levenson, *op. cit.*, p. 64.

11. "Jih-pen kuan k'uei chih erh"; also quoted in "Huai Tung-ching," *Chou Tso-jen tai-piao-tso hsüan*, p. 97.

12. *Ibid.*, p. 99.

13. "Jih-pen chih tsai jen-shih," *Yao-wei-chi*, p. 233; also in "Huai Tung-ching," *Chou Tso-jen tai-piao-tso hsüan*, pp. 97-981. On the Manchu style of dress imposed on the Chinese, see, for instance, Schuyler Camman, *China's Dragon Robes* (New York, 1952), p. 25.

14. "Huai Tung-ching," *Chou Tso-jen tai-piao-tso hsüan*, p. 99.

15. "Jih-pen chih tsai jen-shih," *Yao-wei-chi*, p. 231.

16. "Huai Tung-ching," *Chou Tso-jen tai-piao-tso hsüan*, p. 101.

17. "Sheng-huo chih i-shu," *Chung-kuo hsin-wen-hsüeh ta-hsi*, VII, 163. The same thoughts are elaborated in Chiang Monlin, *op. cit.*, p. 230.

18. "Wo ti tsa-hsüeh," *K'u-k'ou kan-k'ou*, p. 88.

19. On Yen Fu, see ch. III, n. 12.

20. On Lin Shu, see ch. III, n. 11. The reading of Lin Shu's translations is acknowledged by Chou, particularly in his *Chung-kuo hsin-wen-hsüeh ti yüan-liu*, p. 101.

21. See, for instance, *K'u-ch'a sui-pi*, p. 174.

22. Fukuzawa Yukichi (1835–1901) personifies Japanese enlighten-

ment in the early Meiji era, with demands for freedom, equal rights, and rationalism in all fields; see particularly Carmen Blacker, *The Japanese Enlightenment, A Study of the Writings of Fukuzawa Yukichi* (Cambridge, England, 1964).

23. Futabatei Shimei (1864–1909), whose original name was Hasegawa Tatsunosuke, is particularly known for his translations of Turgenev, introducing to Japan the Russian method of psychological analysis; see, e.g., Walter Denning, "Japanese Modern Literature," *Transactions of the Asiatic Society of Japan*, XLI, pt. 1 (1913), 1-186; also *Kindai Nihon bungaku jiten* (Tokyo, 1957), p. 617, and *Kindai bungaku kenkyu hikkei* (Tokyo, 1963), pp. 81-86.

24. Cf. Walter Denning, *op. cit.*, pp. 2-3.

25. In the Preface to his *Hsien-tai Jih-pen hsiao-shuo chi* (Collection of Modern Japanese Short Stories), as quoted in *Chou Tso-jen lun*, p. 184.

26. "Jih-pen chin san-shih nien hsiao-shuo chih fa-ta" (Development of the Short Story in Japan During the Last Thirty Years), *Chung-kuo hsin-wen-hsüeh ta-hsi*, I, 308.

27. For an identification of this office and its functions, see Brunnert and Hagelstrom, *op. cit.*, p. 278.

28. "Huai Tung-ching chih erh," *Yü-chou-feng*, no. 26 (August, 1936); also reprinted in *Chou Tso-jen tai-piao-tso hsüan*, pp. 108-9.

29. *Ibid.*, p. 109. Actually only six volumes of Ellis' *Studies in the Psychology of Sex* had appeared in 1910; the seventh volume was published in 1928. On the occasion of the new 1933 edition of the work, Chou wrote his essay "Hsing ti hsin-li" (Psychology of Sex), August, 1933, contrasting Ellis' thoughts with the behavior of the Nazis, who at that time burned the books and destroyed the Psychological Institute of Dr. Magnus Hirschfeld in Berlin.

30. "Chou Tso-jen tzu-shu," *Chou Tso-jen lun*, p. 2, originally written in 1930 for the *Yen-ta yüeh-k'an*.

31. In his essay "Ai-li-ssu-ti hua'" (Sayings of Ellis), *Yü-t'ien ti shu*, p. 129, Chou Tso-jen says (in 1924): "Havelock Ellis is one of the thinkers I most respect." His admiration for Ellis persisted in later years; see, for instance, Chou's essay "Wo ti ta-hsüeh," ch. XII, where (in 1944) he again praises Ellis as a great thinker and reformer.

32. Su Hsüeh-lin in her article in *Chou Tso-jen lun*, p. 222.

33. "Nan-k'ai chung-hsüeh ti hsing-chiao-yü," *Yü-ssu*, no. 98 (September 25, 1926).

34. "Ch'u yeh-ch'üan hsü-yen," originally written in Japanese, was reprinted in *Yü-ssu*, no. 103 (October 30, 1926).

35. See *Yü-ssu*, no. 73 (April 5, 1926), p. 2, last three lines; also Chou's essay "Chieh-hun ti ai" (Married Love), *Tzu-chi ti yüan-ti*, p. 159.

36. Marie Stopes (1880–1958), a British physician, was best known for her work and writing on "planned parenthood." Her book *Married Love* (1918), subject of one of Chou's essays (see preceding note) was banned in the United States as obscene until 1931; see Keith Briant, *Marie Stopes, a Biography* (London, 1962).

37. See Chou's essay "Ai ti ch'eng-nien" (Love's Coming of Age), *Hsin-ch'ing-nien*, V, no. 4 (October, 1918). This is an essay on Carpenter's book of that title. Similar ideas appear in Chou's essay "Tzu-pen-chu-i ti chin-ch'ang," *T'an-hu-chi*, pp. 83-85, with quotations from Kautsky as further authoritative reference, and "Wen-hsüeh kai-liang yü K'ung-chiao," *Hsin-ch'ing-nien*, V, no. 6, p. 614.

38. The title of Calder-Marshall's book on Ellis, see ch. III, n. 22.

39. Chou Tso-jen's reference to the "part-animal" nature of man induced S. Higuchi to speak of Chou's "biological concept of life"; see S. Higuchi, "Shu Sakujin no seibutsuteki jinkengan ni tsuite," *Kyūshū Chūgoku gakkaihō*, V (1959), 45 ff.

40. "Wo ti tsa-hsüeh," ch. VIII, *K'u-k'ou kan-k'ou*, p. 69. E. A. Westermarck (1862–1939), sociologist, philosopher, and anthropologist, propounded the concept of "ethical relativity," on which Chou commented: "In my old-man's ideology, the only comparatively new element was originally introduced by Yen Fu's so-called *T'ien-yen-lun* [translation of T. H. Huxley's *Evolution and Ethics*], I therefore also came to appreciate the Finnish professor Westermarck's *The Origin and Development of the Moral Idea* [published 1906-8] and feel there are no eternal gospels of earthly righteousness. Morals always undergo changes due to time and place." See *Yü-ssu*, no. 75 (April 16, 1926), 6, lower column. Westermarck is again praised in Chou's essay "Fa hsü chao hsü," *Yü-ssu*, no. 105 (Nov. 13, 1926), 2.

41. *K'u-k'ou kan-k'ou*, p. 67.

42. *Ibid.*, p. 67; see also in "Hsi-su yü shen-hua," *Yeh-tu-ch'ao*, p. 20. Andrew Lang (1844–1912) was a Scottish scholar and novelist, the author of historical fiction and studies of Scottish myths and folk tales; see R. L. Green, *Andrew Lang, a Critical Biography* (Leicester, England, 1946).

43. "Yeh-tu-ch'ao hsiao-yin, *Yeh-tu-ch'ao*, p. 2; also, "Sheng-shu yü Chung-kuo wen-hsüeh," *Hsiao-shuo yüeh-pao*, XII, no. 1 (January 10, 1921), 6; however, a more likely reason is that he was given to believe that a knowledge of Greek mythology was a prerequisite for a deeper understanding of European literature and culture. Indeed, Chou himself gives this explanation in his "Wo ti tsa-hsüeh," ch. VI, and also in "Hsi-la ti yü-kuang, *K'u-k'ou kan-k'ou*, p. 47.

44. "Yeh-tu-ch'ao hsiao-yin," *Yeh-tu-ch'ao*, p. 2.

45. "Fa hsü chao hsü," *Yü-ssu*, no. 105 (November 13, 1926), 2. Morton N. Cohen, *Rider Haggard* (New York, 1960), p. 186, char-

acterizes *The World's Desire* as "a hodgepodge, a ragbag of myth, legend, history, anthropology; Greece, Egypt, and Kor." Twenty-three titles of Haggard's books are listed as translated by Lin Shu in the index *Chin pai-nien lai Chung-i hsi-shu mu-lu* (Index of Western Works Translated into Chinese over the Last Hundred Years) Taipei, 1958), p. 275. Ma T'ai-lai lists twenty-five items; see his "Lin Ch'in-nan so i hsiao-shuo shu-mu," *Ch'u-pan yüeh-k'an*, II, no. 12 (May 1, 1967), 73-74. *Custom and Myth* and *Myth, Ritual, and Religion* are works of Andrew Lang published in London in 1884 and 1887, respectively; the latter is again mentioned by Chou in his essay "Hsi-su yü shen-hua," *Yeh-tu-ch'ao*, p. 20.

46. Among all the writings on ancient Greece, there is an impressive summation of its essence in Walter F. Otto, "Zeit und Antike," *Mythos und Welt* (Stuttgart, 1962), pp. 11-20, which in its formulations is particularly relevant in the present context.

47. Liang Ch'i-ch'ao had been an inspiration to a whole generation of young Chinese, including Chou Tso-jen, and also a guide to a sensible syncretism of Western civilization and Chinese tradition. See J. R. Levenson, *op. cit., esp.* pp. 204-8; also van Boven, *op. cit.,* p. 10.

48. Chang Ping-lin (1869–1936), better known under his courtesy name T'ai-yen, participated in the reform movement and in revolutionary activities in Shanghai at the turn of the century, resulting in his imprisonment and exile to Japan. Chou was particularly impressed with his Chinese classical scholarship and a kind of progressiveness built on Chinese traditional thought, but later resented his attachment to warlord Sun Ch'uan-fang; see "Hsieh pen shih" (1926). On Chang, see particularly Hsü Shou-shang, *Chang Ping-lin* (Shanghai, 1946); also van Boven, *op. cit.,* p. 11, and Michael Gasster, "Currents of Thought in the T'ung-meng-hui," unpubl. diss. (Univ. of Wash., Seattle, 1962), pp. 211-56.

49. *Chung-kuo hsin wen-hsüeh ti yüan-liu,* p. 59: "When I was still small, his influence on me was very great." See also "Chiu jih-chi ch'ao," *Chou Tso-jen tai-piao tso hsüan,* p. 155.

50. The *Shuo-wen,* the full title of which is *Shuo-wen chieh-tzu* (Explaining Simple Graphs and Analysing Compound Graphs), is the work of Hsü Shen (ca. A.D. 100–120), and the earliest Chinese etymological dictionary; cf. Teng and Biggerstaff, *An Annotated Bibliography of Selected Chinese Reference Works* (Cambridge, Mass., 1950), pp. 194-96.

51. Nobori Shōmu (1878–1940); see *Dai jimmei jiten,* IX, 533-44; also see *Kindai Nihon bungaku jiten,* p. 568.

52. Baba Kochō (1869–1940), see *Kindai Nihon bungaku jiten,* p. 582.

53. Published in Tokyo by the T'ung-meng-hui, the revolutionary

party from which the Kuomintang developed; see Chang Ching-lu, *Chung-kuo chin-tai ch'u-pan shih-liao erh-p'ien* (Shanghai, 1954), p. 285; also Michael Gasster, *op. cit.,* pp. 57-59.

54. *Chung-kuo hsin wen-hsüeh ti yüan-liu,* p. 21.

55. *Ibid.,* p. 26.

56. Robert Nisbet Bain (1854–1909) was librarian at the British Museum in London. He published "numerous translations from the Russian, Ruthenian, Roumanian, Hungarian, Swedish, Danish, and Finnish; chiefly fairy tales and novels, 1891–1894." *Who-Was-Who for 1897–1916* (London, 1919), p. 34.

57. "Huang-ch'iang-wei," *Yeh-tu-ch'ao,* p. 8.

58. In 1913, he published a study of children's songs "Erh-ko chih yen-chiu" in a "local magazine"; see "Mi-yu," *Tzu-chi ti yüan-ti,* pp. 48-49. In the same book, p. 254, he mentions that he wrote an article on Sappho for the Shaohsing newspaper *Yü-ch'ang jih-pao.* On the other hand, a collection of Kuei-chi folklore published in 1915 under his name is said to have been compiled by his brother Lu Hsün; see Wang Yeh-ch'iu, *Min-yüan ch'ien ti Lu Hsün hsien-sheng* (n.p., 1947), p. 142.

59. See C. T. Hsia, *A History of Modern Chinese Fiction,* pp. 3-27; Chow Tse-tsung, *The May Fourth Movement,* pp. 269 and 275.

60. See Chow Tse-tsung, *ibid.,* pp. 194-96 and 293-313.

61. K'ang Yu-wei (1858–1927), "the great Chinese reformer and political philosopher of the turn of the century, has been famous as the one great figure of imperial China who made the attempt to transform China within the framework of the Confucian tradition into a society capable of living in the modern world." Franz Michael, Foreword, *K'ang Yu-wei, a Biography and a Symposium,* ed. by Jung-pang Lo (Tucson, 1967).

62. The essay "P'eng shang" is to be found in *T'an-hu-chi,* pp. 45-48, and other publications.

63. *Ibid.,* pp. 9-12, and elsewhere.

64. The *Government Gazette* for the month of March, 1926 (no. 3570), contains the official report on the incident. It names several Communists, among them Li Ta-chao, as instigators of the tumult.

65. "Kuan-yü san-yüeh shih-pa jih ti ssu-che," *Yü-ssu,* no. 72 (March 29, 1926), 3.

66. "Yang chu" (Raising Pigs), *T'an-hu-chi,* p. 219.

67. See *T'an-hu-chi,* p. 223, originally published in *Yü-ssu,* no. 103 (October 30, 1926), 16. The expression *hung-shui meng-shou* (big flood, fierce animal) denoting harm to the people from heretic teachings, goes back to Chu Hsi (1130–1200); cf. Li Chi, *The Use of Figurative Language in Communist China* (Berkeley, 1958), p. 64.

68. "Hei pei-hsin" (Black Vests), *Yü-ssu,* no. 31 (June 15, 1925), 11.

69. *Ibid.*

70. "Kuo-ch'ing-jih" (National Day), *Yü-ssu,* no. 101 (October 16, 1926), 18.

71. *Yung-jih-chi,* p. 266.

72. "Kuo-ch'ing-jih sung" (In Praise of National Day), *Yung-jih-chi,* pp. 264-70. On p. 264, Chou quotes a decision of the National Government at its Ninety-eighth Meeting designating the day as Confucius Day.

73. "Kuo-ch'ing-jih sung," *Yung-jih-chi,* p. 269.

74. Cf. Chow Tse-tsung, *op. cit.,* pp. 289-90.

75. This was a widely held conviction; see, for instance, Chow Tse-tsung, "The Anti-Confucian Movement in Early Republican China," *The Confucian Persuasion,* ed. by A. F. Wright (Stanford, 1960), pp. 288-375.

76. "Tsu-hsien ch'ung-pai" (Ancestor Worship), *T'an-hu-chi,* p. 2.

77. The *san-kang* seem to have been first formulated in the *Wei-han wen-chia,* an apocryphal commentary to the *Li-chi* (Book of Rites); see Morohashi, *Dai Kan-Wa jiten,* I, p. 115. They occupy considerable space in the *Po-hu-t'ung* discussions of the classics (A.D. 79); cf. Tjan Tsoe Som, *Po Hu T'ung* (Leiden, 1949), pp. 559-64, and ever since formed an important element of Confucian dogma. The first weighty criticism of this system in modern times was Chang Chih-tung's *Ch'üan-hsüeh-p'ien;* see particularly the chapter entitled "Ming kang" (Elucidating the Relationships). An English translation of Chang's work is S. I. Woodbridge's *China's Only Hope* (New York, 1900). During the May Fourth Movement, the attack against the system was renewed by Ch'en Tu-hsiu in his "Hsien-fa yü K'ung-chiao" (Constitution and Confucianism), *Hsin-ch'ing-nien,* II, no. 3 (November, 1916), 1-5. For a more recent, informative article on the *san-kang,* see Chester C. Tan, "Tradition and the New Culture," *Tsing Hua Journal of Chinese Studies,* II, no. 1 (May 1960), 287-99.

78. The *wu-lun,* or Five (Cardinal Human) Relations, was first defined in the *Meng-tzu* (see Legge, *The Four Books,* p. 128), which cites them as concepts of the mythical emperor Shun. They were first designated as such in the Ming dynasty in the primer *Wu-lun-shih* by Shen I, and later made the title of a book, the *Wu-lun-shu* compiled by the Ming emperor Hsüantsung (1425–34); see Morohashi, *op. cit.,* I, p. 514, under "Wu-lun," "Wu-lun-shih," and "Wu-lun-shu."

79. Chou Tso-jen wrote on this aspect of the *wu-lun* in his essay "Wo ti tsa-hsüeh," ch. IX, *K'u-k'ou kan-k'ou,* p. 71. The idea was already pointed out by Chang Chih-tung in his *Ch'üan-hsüeh-p'ien,* ch. III.

80. "Tsu-hsien ch'ung-pai" (Ancestor Worship), *T'an-hu-chi*, p. 1.

81. A strong influence of Herbert Spencer is visible here; cf. Spencer, "The Origin of Animal Worship," *Essays* (New York, 1910), I, pp. 309-10.

82. *T'an-hu-chi*, p. 1.

83. "Chia chih shang-hsia ssu-p'ang," *Chou Tso-jen tai-piao-tso hsüan*, p. 74. Cf. *Lun-yü*, XVI, 13: "That the superior man maintains a distant reserve towards his son."

84. For translations of *Twenty-Four Examples of Filial Piety*, see John C. Ferguson, *Mythology of All Races* (Boston, 1928), VIII, pp. 160-66, and *Chinese Repository*, VI (1838), 130-42; also: Alfred Koehn, *Piété Filiale en Chine* (Peking, 1944); M. Titiev and Hsing-chih Tien, "A Primer of Filial Piety," *Papers of the Michigan Academy of Science, Art, and Letters*, XXXII (1947), 259-66, which translates fifteen of the stories, illustrated with the original Chinese woodcuts. James Legge describes the *T'ai-shang kan-ying p'ien* in the Introduction to his *Texts of Taoism*, in F. Max Muller, ed., *Sacred Books of the East*, XXXIX (Oxford, 1891), pp. 38-40, and translated it into English, *ibid.*, XL, pp. 235-46; see also Holmes Welch, *Taoism, the Parting of the Way*, rev. ed. (Boston, 1966), pp. 139-41.

85. *Yang chih* here stands for "nurturing the wishes of one's parents," to give delight and comfort to the parents by not only satisfying their physical needs, but also by "ministering to their heart"; W. A. C. H. Dobson, *Mencius* (Toronto, 1963), p. 139. The term originates from Mencius' praise of Tseng-tzu; see *Meng-tzu*, "Li-lou, shang," 19, in Legge, *The Chinese Classics*, Hong Kong, 1960 ed., II, p. 310, to which Chu Hsi added the gloss: *ch'eng shun fu-mu chih* (to satisfy the parents' wishes), as, e.g., in the *Ssu-pu pei-yao* edition of *Meng-tzu* with Chu Hsi's commentary.

86. "Chia chih shang-hsia ssu-p'ang," *Chou Tso-jen tai-piao-tso hsüan*, p. 75.

87. "T'i Wei Wei-nung hsien-sheng chia shu hou," *Yeh-tu-ch'ao*, pp. 306-7.

88. In *Tzu-chi ti yüan-ti*, p. 106.

89. *Ibid.*, p. 111.

90. *Chung-kuo hsin-wen-hsüeh ta-hsi*, VII, p. 106.

91. *Ibid.*, p. 134.

92. Albert Mordell, *The Erotic Motive in Literature* (New York, 1919).

93. The *ssu-k'u* (four storehouses/sections of a library) is the traditional Chinese library classification with four main classes: Classics, History, Philosophers, and Literature. The *tzu* section referred to by Chou Tso-jen is the third class, containing the commentators and exegetists of the classics; cf. Kang Woo, *Histoire de la*

Bibliographie Chinoise (Paris, 1938), pp. 21-37; A. Wylie, *Notes on Chinese Literature*, pp. 81 ff.

94. "I-yü yü Lun-yü," *Chou Tso-jen tai-piao-tso hsüan*, p. 265.

95. "Mei-hua-ts'ao-t'ang pi-t'an teng," *Chou Tso-jen tai-piao-tso hsüan*, p. 160.

96. "I-yü yü Lun-yü," *Chou Tso-jen tai-piao-tso hsüan*, p. 266. The Chinese expressions used in the original text are *ju-chia* (*ju* scholar) and *ju-chiao-t'u* (follower of the teachings/religion of Confucius). The translations "confucian" and "confucianist" are suggested in a similar context by Chow Tse-tsung, "The Anti-Confucian Movement in Early Republican China," *The Confucian Persuasion*, p. 370, n. 7.

97. See, for instance, Max Wundt, *Die deutsche Schulphilosophie im Zeitalter der Aufklärung* (Tübingen, 1945), pp. 176-77; also Wolfgang Franke, *China und das Abendland* (Göttingen, 1962), p. 53; Otto Franke, "Leibniz und China," *Aus Kultur und Geschichte Chinas* (Peking, 1945), pp. 313-30; H. G. Creel, *Confucius, the Man and the Myth* (New York, 1949), p. 271.

98. "Confucius became one of the patron saints of the Enlightenment," says A. H. Rawbotham in "Oriental-Western Cultural Relations in a Changing World," *Indiana University Conference on Oriental-Western Literary Relations* (Chapel Hill, 1955), p. 209.

99. "Lüeh t'an Chung-Hsi wen-hsüeh," *Jen-chien-shih*, Hankow ed., no. 1 (March 16, 1936).

100. "Ch'ing-li" (Reason) in *Chih-t'ang wei-k'an-kao* (Unpublished Works of Chou Tso-jen) (Amherst, Mass., 1965), p. 5a; see also *K'u-ch'a sui-pi*, p. 338; similarly, Hu Shih, "Scientific Spirit and Method in Chinese Philosophy," *Philosophy and Culture East and West* (Honolulu, 1962), pp. 199-222.

101. On Hsün-tzu, originally named Hsün K'uang, third-century B.C. Confucian philosopher, see particularly H. H. Dubs, *Hsüntze, the Moulder of Ancient Confucianism* (London, 1927). The words cited by Chou Tso-jen appear in *Hsün-tzu*, ch. VI; see Concordance to *Hsün-tzu* in the Harvard-Yenching Sinological Index Series, suppl. XX, p. 16, line 2.

102. The *Hou Han-shu* (History of the Later Han Dynasty) records the story of Yang Chen (d. A.D. 124) who was proferred a bribe in the dark so that nobody would know. His reply was: "Heaven knows, Earth knows, you will know, and I shall know"; see H. A. Giles, *Chinese Biographical Dictionary*, p. 895. In reference to this story, Yang Hsi-fu (1701-68) chose or was given the studio name "Ssu-chih t'ang" ("Four-know," or "Four Knowledge/Wisdom" Studio).

103. At the end of Preface to *K'an-yün-chi*.

104. See especially E. H. von Tscharner, "Menschseins-Ideale in

den orientalischen Kulturen; China," *Asiatische Studien,* XIII (1960), 99 ff. Also see Chan Wing-tsit, "Chinese Theory and Practice with Special Reference to Humanism," *Philosophy and Culture East and West* (Honolulu, 1962), pp. 81-95, particularly p. 85: "It was Confucius, of course, who brought Chinese humanism to its climax"; and p. 88: "His [Confucius'] humanism is complete." The same author gives a historical study of *jen* in "The Concept of Jen," *The Concept of Man* (Lincoln, Nebraska, 1960), pp. 183-88.

105. "Chung-kuo ti ssu-hsiang wen-t'i" (1942), *Yao-t'ang tsa-wen,* p. 10.

106. "The concept of *jen,* variously translated as 'benevolence,' 'love,' 'altruism,' 'human-heartedness,' 'man-to-manness,' and so forth, is the backbone of Confucianism. In the *Analects,* 58 of the 499 chapters are devoted to its discussion, and the word appears 105 times," Chan Wing-tsit, "K'ang Yu-wei and the Confucian Doctrine of Humanity (Jen)," *K'ang Yu-wei; a Biography and a Symposium* (Tucson, 1967), pp. 355-74.

107. Cf. Ezra Pound in the "Terminology" that precedes the text of his *Confucius, the Great Digest and Unwobbling Pivot* (London, 1952), p. 22; *"Jen,* Humanitas, humanity, in the full sense of the word, 'manhood,' the man and his full contents."

108. To mention here one significant incident: when Chou Tso-jen was asked to inscribe a souvenir scroll at the Atarashiki Mura settlement (see ch. I, n. 28), he quoted the *Lun-yü,* VII, 29, which in translation read: "Is *jen* a thing remote? I wish to be *jen,* and lo: *jen* is at hand." (Cf. Legge, *The Four Books,* p. 68). The incident is recorded in Chou's "Jih-hsiang hsin-ts'un" (The "New Village" at Hyuga), *Hsin-ch'ao,* II, no. 1 (April, 1919), 78.

109. "Wo ti tsa-hsüeh," ch. IV, *K'u-k'ou kan-k'ou,* p. 60. In the same sense, he speaks of Ts'ai Yüan-p'ei as a real *ju-chia;* see "Chi Ts'ai Chieh-min hsien-sheng ti shih," *Ku-chin,* no. 6 (August, 1942).

110. H. G. Creel has to some extent repudiated opinions expressed in his *Sinism; a Study of the Evolution of the Chinese World-View* (Chicago, 1929); see his *Confucius, the Man and the Myth,* p. 306, n. 4; nevertheless, some formulations seem valid and relevant in this connection, as, e.g., p. 120: "Sinism is not the chance creation of a handful of Chinese intellectuals led by Confucius, but . . . rather the expression, in philosophical form, of the historically evolved world-view of the Chinese people." A similar thought seems to have motivated R. Wilhelm to say: "Taoism was not founded by Lao-tzu, neither was Confucianism founded by Confucius. Both of them, Lao-tzu and Confucius, have their footing in Chinese antiquity." See his "On the Sources of Chinese Taoism," *Journal of the Royal Asiatic*

Society, North-China Branch, XLV (1914), 2; see also Hu Shih, "Shuo ju" (Speaking of *ju*) *in Hu Shih wen-ts'un,* IV, pp. 1-103.

111. This trend toward syncretism was strong throughout the whole Chinese reform movement, right up to very recent times. G. K. Kindermann in his *Konfuzianimus, Sunyatsenismus und chinesischer Kommunismus* (Freiburg, 1963), p. 62, reports, for instance, on a Communist symposium on Confucianism in 1962, when much "advanced ideology" was read out of Confucius' works. See also Hellmut Wilhelm, "The Problem of Within and Without, a Confucian Attempt in Syncretism," *Journal of the History of Ideas,* XII, no. 1 (January, 1951), 48-60; H. G. Creel, *Chinese Thought from Confucius to Mao Tse-tung* (Chicago, 1953); Chan Wing-tsit reviewing Feng Yu-lan's *Chung-kuo che-hsüeh-shih hsin-pien* in *Journal of Asian Studies,* XXIV, 495-97.

112. See particularly F. E. A. Krause, *Ju-Tao-Fo, die religiösen und philosophischen Systeme Ostasiens* (Munich, 1924), p. 452; also Nakamura Hajime, *Ways of Thinking of Eastern People: India-China-Japan* (Honolulu, 1964), p. 287.

113. This refers to a famous Buddhist layman by the name of Yang Wen-hui (1837–1911), whose courtesy name was Jen-shan; see Chan Wing-tsit, *Religious Trends in Modern China* (New York, 1953), p. 60; also *Shih-yung Fo-hsüeh tz'u-tien* (A Practical Dictionary of Buddhism) (Shanghai, 1935), pp. 1544-45. A short note on him may also be found in his granddaughter's book *I-ko nü-jen ti tzu-chuan* (Autobiography of a Woman) by Yang Pu-wei (Mrs. Chao Yuenren) (Taipei, 1967), p. 83.

114. E. T. C. Werner, *Dictionary of Chinese Mythology,* p. 28.

115. "Wo ti tsa-hsüeh," ch. XIX, *K'u-k'ou Kan-k'ou,* p. 91.

116. *Ibid.,* p. 90. It is also interesting to note in this connection that he had prepared a course on the literature of the Buddhist texts in 1937, when the Japanese closed the university; see *ibid.,* p. 91.

177. "Chieh yüan tou," *Chou Tso-jen tai-piao-tso hsüan,* pp. 77-81.

118. See G. Willoughby-Meade, "Chinese Buddhism of Today," *Chinese Ghouls and Goblins,* pp. 69-101.

119. For instance, the adverse effect of popular Buddhist literature on the minds of uneducated young women is criticized by Chou in his "Nü-tzu ti ch'u-lu," *Yü-chou-feng,* no. 21.

120. See particularly C. B. Day, *Chinese Peasant Cults* (Shanghai, 1940), pp. 175-76, with several references to other literature on this question; also G. Willoughby-Meade, "Popular Taoism: The Craft of the Wizard and the Fortune-Teller," *Chinese Ghouls and Goblins,* pp. 47-68; cf. also R. Wilhelm, "On the Sources of Chinese Taoism," p. 1: "Taoism so far as it is original is no religion, so far as it is a religion, it is not original."

121. *Lun-yü,* III, 12.

122. "Hsiang-ts'un yü Tao-chiao ssu-hsiang," *Chou Tso-jen wen-hsüan,* p. 165, of which part one was originally published in *Hsin-sheng-huo* (1920), and part two in *Yü-ssu,* no. 100 (October 23, 1926).

123. Note the almost identical expression used by Dr. Wu Lien-te, the famous public health pioneer of modern China in the *Chinese Recorder* (of August, 1936), as quoted by E. R. Hughes, *The Invasion of China by the Western World* (London, 1937), p. 221.

124. See Chang Chih-tung, Chapter "Hsün hsü," in his *Ch'üan hsüeh p'ien.* Hsüeh Chün-tu translates the phrase in question as "Chinese learning for the fundamental principles, Western learning for practical application," in his *Huang Hsing and the Chinese Revolution* (Stanford, 1961), p. 4.

125. *Yung-jih-chi,* pp. 206-7.

126. We also find similar ideas expressed by Liang Ch'i-ch'ao; see Joseph R. Levenson, *op. cit.,* p. 48.

127. Francis L. K. Hsü, *Religion, Science, and Human Crisis* (London, 1952), pp. 36-38 and 135-37.

128. *Yung-jih-chi,* p. 211.

129. Chow Tse-tsung, *op. cit.,* pp. 282-83; J. Lust, "The Su-pao Case," *Bulletin of the School of Oriental and African Languages,* XXVI (1964), pt. 2, 408-29; Chao Ts'ung, *Wu-ssu wen-t'an tien-ti* (Hong Kong, 1964), pp. 81-82 and 114. On Chang's relations to Lu Hsün, see also W. Schultz, *op. cit.,* p. 377. For a short biographical sketch, see *Chung-kuo hsin-wen-hsüeh ta-hsi,* X, p. 222, with further references quoted there; also, Huo I-hsien, *Tsui-chin erh-shih-nien Chung-kuo wen-hsüeh-shih kang* (Canton, 1936), p. 27. For a more recent characterization of Chang Shih-chao, see Ch'en Ching-shih's article in *Ch'ang-liu,* XXXI, no. 11 (Taipei; July 16, 1965), 4-6.

130. "Sheng-shu yü Chung-kuo wen-hsüeh," *Hsiao-shuo yüeh-pao,* XII, no. 1, (January 1921), 4-5, where he states that Jesus' teachings are the source of modern humanitarianism; also see Chou's article in the *Sheng-ming yüeh-k'an* quoted by L. Wieger, *Remours et Écume,* p. 23. Even Ch'en Tu-hsiu was an admirer of Jesus in this sense; see Chow Tse-tsung, *op. cit.,* p. 321. An interesting attempt to equate the Chinese tradition with certain aspects of Christinanity (e.g., *agape=jen*) from the Christian point of view is Leo Sherley-Prince, *Confucius and Christ* (New York, 1951).

131. "Ch'i-lu" (Crossroads), a poem in *Hsiao-shuo yüeh-pao,* XIII, no. 4 (April, 1922).

132. "Jen ti wen-hsüeh," *Hsin-ch'ing-nien,* V, no. 6 (December 15, 1919).

133. *China Year Book 1928,* p. 1333. Wolfgang Franke, "Die anti-

christliche Bewegung," *Das Jahrhundert der chinesischen Revolution,* pp. 216-21. Also K. S. Latourette, "The Anti-Christian Movement," in his *A History of Christian Missions in China* (London, 1929).

134. Harold Acton, "The Creative Spirit in Modern Chinese Literature," *T'ien Hsia Monthly,* I, no. 4 (November, 1935), 377.

135. Liang Ch'i-ch'ao was also among those intellectuals who voiced their opposition to the anti-Christian movement; see Y. Y. Tsu, "Spiritual Tendencies of the Chinese People as Shown Outside of the Christian Church Today," *The Chinese Recorder,* LVI, no. 12 (December, 1925), 777. On Chou Tso-jen's attitude, see Chan Wing-tsit, *Religious Trends in Modern China* (New York, 1953), pp. 227, 230-32.

136. See Chou's article in *Sheng-ming yüeh-k'an* referred to in fn. 130 above.

137. James George Frazer, *Psyche's Task* (London, 1913), which was reissued in 1927 under the title *The Devil's Advocate.*

138. "Shen-hua yü ch'uan-shuo," *Tzu-chi ti yüan-ti,* p. 37.

139. *K'ung-ta-ku,* p. 207; *Yung-jih-chi,* pp. 45-76, 76-78, and 97-101.

140. See list of contents of *Yü-ssu,* 1934–27 issues, in *Chung-kuo hsin wen-hsüeh ta-hsi,* X, pp. 487-504.

141. *T'an-hu-chi,* p. 195.

142. *Kuo-ch'ü ti kung-tso,* p. 48.

143. *Yung-jih-chi,* pp. 132-48, as "Ai-li-ssu kan-hsiang lu ch'ao," *ibid.,* p. 252; and also *Tzu-chi ti yüan-ti,* p. 91.

144. Both are in the collection *Ming-shih lü-hsing.*

145. The two stories were entiled "Pu-tzu-jan t'ao-t'ai" (Unnatural Elimination) and "Kai-ko" (Reform) in Chinese translation, when they first appeared in the *Hsin-ch'ing-nien* (1918) and later in the collection *K'ung-ta-ku* (1928).

146. See *Tien-ti* and *K'ung ta-ku.*

147. Yang Liang-kung, a former student of Chou's at National Peking University, called the textbook "dry and without flavor" in a recent article "Wu nien ta-hsüeh sheng-huo" (Five Years of University Life), *Chuan-chi wen-hsüeh,* IV, no. 1 (January, 1964).

148. These essays (dated 1918–23), are all in *I-shu yü sheng-huo.*

149. See n. 27 to ch. I.

150. See, e.g., "T'an Jih-pen wen-hua shu, ch'i erh," *Kua-tou-chi,* pp. 80-81.

151. See *T'an-hu-chi,* pp. 19-20. The article was originally published in the Peking *Ch'en-pao* (newspaper), as Chou claimed in his "Jih-pen kuan k'uei chih san."

152. "Jih-pen yü Chung-kuo," *Chung-kuo hsin-wen-hsüeh ta-hsi,* VII, p. 226. The article was first published in the *Ching-pao* newspaper

of October 10, 1925 (see, "Jih-pen lang-jen yü Shun-t'ien shih-pao", *Yü-ssu*, no. 51).

153. E. B. Ceadel, "Japanese Literature" in *Literatures of the East; an Appreciation* (London, 1953), pp. 165-68. A less sympathetic treatment is to be found in W. G. Aston, *A History of Japanese Literature* (London, 1899), pp. 17-48.

154. This novel is well described in W. G. Aston, *ibid.*, pp. 92-103. It has been translated as *The Tale of Genji* by Arthur Waley (Boston, 1926).

155. "Wen-ming-kuo ti wen-tzu-yü," *Chou Tso-jen wen-hsüan*, pp. 25-29.

156. In *Yung-jih-chi*, p. 238.

157. "P'ai Jih ti ou-hua" (Worsening of the Hatred against Japan), *T'an-hu-chi*, pp. 17-18.

158. *K'u-ch'a sui-pi*, pp. 241-42, where he makes particular reference to the narcotics trade carried on by Japanese or persons under Japanese protection; cf. G. E. Taylor, *The Struggle for North China*, p. 150.

159. "Jih-pen yü Chung-kuo," *Chung-kuo hsin-wen-hsüeh ta-hsi*, VII, p. 228. He assailed the *Shun-t'ien shih-pao*, a Japanese newspaper printed in China, for displaying this unwholesome *Chih-na-t'ung* spirit. See also "Jih-pen lang-jen yü Shun-t'ien shih-pao," *Yü-ssu*, no. 51 (November, 1925).

160. In *Chou Tso-jen wen-hsüan*, pp. 50-51. A similar case is dealt with in his "Ch'ing-p'u tzu-chüeh chih t'e-shu li-chieh" (The Special Understanding of Viscount Kiyoura), *Yü-ssu*, no. 102.

161. Yasuoka Hideo, *Shōsetsu kara mita Shina no minzoku-shi* (Tokyo, 1925).

162. *Chou Tso-jen wen-hsüan*, p. 51.

163. "Liu-hsüeh ti hui-i," *Yao-t'ang tsa-wen*, p. 96.

164. "Ming-chih wen-hsüeh ti hui-i," *Li-ch'un i-ch'ien*, pp. 70-75.

165. Kunikida Doppo (1871–1908); see *Kindai Nihon bungaku jiten*, p. 265.

166. Natsume Sōseki (1867–1916); *ibid.*, p. 546.

167. Mori Ōgai (1862–1922); *ibid.*, p. 710. At the time of Ōgai's death, Chou wrote a eulogy; see *T'an-lung-chi*, pp. 37-43.

168. Arishima Takeo (1878–1923), see *Kindai Nihon bungaku jiten*, p. 87. A eulogy on Arishima is contained in Chou's *T'an-lung-chi*, pp. 45-48, which was written in July, 1923.

169. See, for instance, the translations of selected representative modern Japanese short stories in Richard N. McKinnon, ed., *The Heart Is Alone* (Tokyo, 1957), and Donald Keene, *Modern Japanese Literature; an Anthology* (New York, 1956).

170. Yosano Akiko (1878–1942), the best known of early modern

women writers; see *Kindai Nihon bungaku jiten,* p. 745. Chou wrote a eulogy on hearing of her death and included it in his *K'u-ch'a sui-pi,* pp. 173-77.

171. Chou's translation "Chen-ts'ao lun" (On Chastity), *Hsin ch'ing-nien,* IV, no. 5 (May 15, 1918), is acclaimed for its humane spirit by Hu shih in the same magazine, V, no. 1 (see "Chen-ts'ao wen-t'i").

172. Bakin (1767–1848), whose full name was Takizawa Bakin, was one of the greatest Japanese novelists. His heroes and heroines were "grotesque and unreal"; see W. G. Aston, *op. cit.,* pp. 352-56, and *Nihon bungaku daijiten,* 1934 ed., III, pp. 325-28.

173. *Haibun* is a mixture of *haiku* poetry with prose. For a biography of Kobayashi Issa (1763-1827), see *Haikai and Haiku* (Tokyo, 1958), pp. 159-60. Translations of Issa's poetry were published under the title *The Years of My Life* by Noboyuki Yuasa (Berkeley, 1960), and into German by G. S. Dombrady, *Kobayashi Issa's Ora ga Haru* (Wiesbaden, 1959).

174. Ishikawa Takuboku (1886–1912), see *Kindai Nihon bungaku jiten,* p. 101. Chou's essay is called 'Shih-ch'uan Cho-mu ti tuan-ko" (Ishikawa Takuboku's *Tanka*), *Hsiao-shuo yüeh-pao,* XIV, no. 1 (January, 1923).

175. Shimazaki Tōson (1872–1943), see *Nihon bungakushi jiten,* pp. 383-89. Chou Tso-jen's article—actually a eulogy on the poet and novelist—is to be found in the *I-wen tsa-chih,* I, no. 4 (October, 1943), and was later included in *Yao-t'ang tsa-wen,* pp. 111-14.

176. *Hsin ch'ing-nien,* V, no. 1 (July 15, 1918), 27-42.

177. The *kyōgen* are comical interludes between the serious, often tragic, *noh* plays. For a bibliography on the *kyōgen,* see B. S. Silberman, *Japan and Korea, a Critical Bibliography* (Tucson, 1962), pp. 61-62. Chou Tso-jen's translations of *kyōgen* plays were published under the title *K'uang-yen shih-fan* (Ten Kyōgen Plays) (Peking, 1926).

178. In issues 65, 69, 71, and 78 (all 1926) of the *Yü-ssu* magazine, under the heading "Han i ku-shih-chi shen-tai chüan." Professor K. Ando reports in the *Daian* monthly of January, 1964, p. 6, that he was presented with a copy of a complete translation of the *Kojiki* prepared by Chou and published by Jen-min wen-hsüeh-she (Peking, 1962).

179. See particularly the introduction (p. ix–xxv) to *Haikai and Haiku;* also see R. H. Blyth, *A History of Haiku* (Tokyo, 1963).

180. On the *kyōku* and *senryu,* see *Nihon bungaku daijiten,* 4th ed. (1935), II pp. 840-41. See also R. H. Blyth, *Senryu, Japanese Satirical Verses* (Tokyo, 1950).

181. "Jih-pen shih-jen I-ch'a ti shih," *Hsiao-shuo yüeh-pao,* XII, no. 11 (November, 1929).

182. The expression "leaf on the waves" to signify a small boat is a frequently used term in traditional Chinese poetry. Morohashi, *op. cit.*, I, 4, quotes examples from Han Yü (768–824), Li Shang-yin (783–858), Su Shih (1037–1101), and Wang An-shih (1021–86).

183. Lan-t'ing (Orchid Pavillion) was the scene of an outing of literary friends immortalized by Wang Hsi-chih's essay; see n. 9, ch. II.

184. This plant is identified by its scientific name *ficus pumila* in K'ung Ch'ing-lai, *Chih-wu-hsüeh ta tz'u-tien* (Botanical Dictionary) (Shanghai, 1930), p. 1438, which is translated as "Dwarf Fig Tree" in Loudon's *Encyclopaedia of Plants* (London, 1866), p. 872.

185. The letter appears as an essay under the title "Wu-p'eng ch'uan" (Black Awning Boat) in *Yü-ssu*, no. 107 (November 27, 1926), 4-6. It has been reprinted many times, most recently in *Ch'un-wen-hsüeh*, II, no. 1 (July, 1967), 38-40, and in a textbook for Chinese junior middle school students, *Ch'u-chung kuo-wen* (Peking, 1939), pp. 108-113. For a short description of these boats, see Jen Wei-yin, *Shao-hsing san chi* (Random Notes on Shaohsing) (Shanghai, 1956), pp. 7-8.

186. "T'an Mu-lien hsi," *T'an-lung-chi*, pp. 137-42; also *Chung-kuo hsin-wen-hsüeh ti yüan-liu*, pp. 26-27.

187. The term "teaism," that Chou quotes here, seems to have been coined by K. Okakura, *The Book of Tea* (New York, 1906), p. 1, where he defines it further as "a religion of aestheticism, the adoration of the beautiful among everyday facts."

188. George Robert Gissing (1857–1903), an English novelist, whose novel *The Private Papers of Henry Ryecroft* was first published in 1903.

189. The passage referred to actually reads: "Is it believable that the Chinese, in who knows how many centuries, have derived from tea a millionth part of the pleasure or the good which it has brought to England in the past one hundred years?" See, G. R. Gissing, *op. cit.* 1953 ed., p. 183.

190. K. Okakura, *op. cit.* A Chinese translation of this book was prepared by Fang Chi-sheng and published with a foreword by Chou Tso-jen dated November 20, 1944; cf. Chou's *Li-ch'un i-ch'ien*, pp. 188-90.

191. K. Okakura, *op. cit.*, p. 27.

192. The *po-po* is a North Chinese variety of cake made of wheat flour or Indian corn. L. Woitsch, "Beiträge zur Lexikographie des Chinesischen," *Acta Orientalia*, 1924, p. 233, lists a type called *Man-chou po-po* (Manchu dumplings), while *Man-Han po-po*, as Chou calls them, may be translated "Manchu-Chinese dumplings."

193. This seems to be a transcription of a southern pronunciation of

what in North China is known as the *wo-wo-t'ou,* a kind of dumpling.

194. Ueda Kyōsuke (1871–1951) was an expert on ceramics, but also on things Chinese, as shown in his book *Shumi no Shina sōdan* (Interesting China Talk) (Tokyo, 1925); also see *Bunka jimmei roku 1963,* p. 4530.

195. *Yang-kan-ping* (Sheep-liver pastry), presumably so called due to its color and appearance, is mentioned as a special food prepared at Loyang on the Ch'ung-yang festival (9th of the 9th month); see Morohashi, *op. cit.,* IX, p. 50.

196. On the Japanese monk Taku'an Hōshi (1573–1645), see *Nihon bungaku daijiten* (Tokyo, 1934–36), XVII, p. 6; also E. Papinot, *Historical and Geographical Dictionary of Japan* (Tokyo, 1909), p. 640.

Chapter Six

1. At one time, even the harmless book *Tzu-chi ti yüan-ti* (Our Own Garden) was banned by the metropolitan police of Peking as "subversive"; see *Chung-kuo hsin-wen-hsüeh ta-hsi,* VII, p. 261, and Yin Fa-lu, "Pei-yang chün-fa tui chin-pu k'an-wu ts'ui-ts'an" (Suppression of Progressive Publications by the North China Warlords) in *Chung-kuo hsien-tai ch'u-pan shih-liao, chia pien,* pp. 50-54.

2. See, for instance, Franklin W. Houn, *Central Government of China 1912–1928; an Institutional Study* (Madison, 1957), pp. 157-59.

3. Lu Hsün, for instance, left Peking in August, 1926, and finally took up residence in the French Concession of Shanghai. Also see Huo I-hsien, *Tsui-chin erh-shih nien Chung-kuo wen-hsüeh shih-kang* (Canton, 1936), p. 38.

4. *K'u-ch'a sui-pi,* p. 160.

5. Huo I-hsien, *op. cit.,* pp. 38-39 and 54.

6. See, for instance, *Kuo-ch'ü ti kung-tso,* p. 73.

7. "He would rather be a lonely recluse in his studio than become one of the great demagogues peddling Marxism or the ideas of Nietzsche," says Su Hsüeh-lin in her "Chou Tso-jen hsien-sheng yen-chiu," *Chou Tso-jen lun,* p. 212.

8. *Yung-jih-chi,* pp. 255-62.

9. Published in the first issue of *Jen-chien-shih,* April 5, 1934, in facisimile, as addressed by Chou to his friend and editor of this magazine, Lin Yutang. Chou calls them *ta-yu* poems, that is, rhymes in the colloquial so named after the T'ang dynasty poet Chang Ta-yu.

10. The first line is a reference to a family superstition that Chou must have been a monk in a former existence; see *Li-ch'un i-ch'ien,* p.

69; also Ts'ao Chü-jen, "Ts'ung K'ung-jung tao T'ao Yüan-ming ti lu," *Chou Tso-jen lun,* p. 70.

11. The common saying is "hua she t'ien tsu" (paint a snake and add legs) as an expression of something superfluous and useless; see C. A. S. Williams, *A Manual of Chinese Metaphor* (Shanghai, 1920), p. 203.

12. This seems to allude to a scene in the novel *Erh-shih nien mu-tu chih kuai hsien-chuang* (Curious Things Observed in Twenty Years) by Wu Wo-yao (1867–1910), where, toward the end of ch. VI, the impoverished scholar slaps the table, as if suddenly struck by an idea, but actually to make sesame seeds which he eats, jump out of fissures in the table. The meaning of the allusion is to attempt to maintain the façade of a well-to-do existence while actually in dire financial straits.

13. *Chou Tso-jen lun,* p. 37.

14. Ts'ao Chü-jen, *op. cit.,* p. 70. See also Hsü Chieh, *ibid.,* pp. 33-34, where he quotes Hu Feng:" the translator of Yaroshenko's 'Spirit of the Past' has now himself become a spirit of the past."

16. See Hsü Chieh, *ibid.,* p. 33. Only six out of the original eight lines are quoted.

17. The two quoted phrases refer to the titles of two of Chou's books, namely, *K'an-yün-chi* and *K'u-ch'a sui-pi.*

18. The Chinese expression used here literally means "those who have lived before Emperor Fu Hsi." The ancients were said to have lived with the utmost unconcern for everything around them. The poet T'ao Yüan-ming also applied the expression to himself.

19. Huo I-hsien, *Tsui-chin erh-shih nien Chung-kuo wen-hsüeh shih-kang,* p. 111.

20. Quoted in *Chou Tso-jen lun,* p. 34; also mentioned on p. 61.

21. *Chung-kuo hsin-wen-hsüeh ta-hsi,* II, *tao yen,* p. 14, also quoted in Huo I-hsien, *op. cit.,* p. 112.

22. "Kuan-yü k'u ch'a." *K'u-ch'a sui-pi,* p. 1.

23. Isaac Goldberg, *op. cit.,* p. 88. Chou's remarks are in "Tse-hsieh-chi hsü"; they are also quoted in *Chou Tso-jen lun,* p. 5.

24. When Chou Tso-jen stood trial for treason, the Shanghai *Ta-kung-pao* (October 25, 1946) published a long article on Chou's wartime writings: Huang Po-ssu, "Chou Tso-jen ti chi pen shu" (Some Books by Chou Tso-jen).

25. Some of the titles, like *The Gods and Heroes of Greece, Aesop's Fables, The Comedies of Aristophanes, The Greek Poetess Sappho,* published 1952–55, were soon reported to be unobtainable in the Hong Kong book market, which suggests that even these translations may perhaps have been ideologically unwelcome and thus refused export by the Communist authorities.

Chapter Seven

1. In 1932, Chou Tso-jen was asked to lecture at Fu Jen University, Peking, on the Chinese literary tradition. His lecture notes were later edited and published as a booklet under the title *Chung-kuo hsin-wen-hsüeh ti yüan-liu* (Sources of China's New Literature). A Hong Kong book company republished it in 1955 under the title *Chung-kuo chin-tai wen-hsüeh shih-hua* (On the History of China's Modern Literature).

2. The origin of the two terms *yen-chih* and *tsai-tao* can be explained as follows: *Shih-yen-chih* (poetry expresses sentiment) first appears in the section "Shun-t'ien" of the *Shu-ching* classic, as part of the instructions the great emperor Shun gave to his master of music. The phrase was then further elaborated to *shih-che chih chih so chih yeh* (poetry is the product of emotions/sentiment) in the Great Preface to the *Shih-ching* classic; this preface is believed to have been written by Wei Hung (fl. A.D. 25). Cf. Chu Tzu-ch'ing, *Shih-chih-pien* (Taipei, 1964). *Wen i tsai tao* (literature is the vehicle of the *tao*) seems to have evolved in this phrasing during the T'ang and Sung dynasties; see Kuo Shao-yü, *Chung-kuo wen-hsüeh p'i-p'ing shih*, p. 200; cf. also Vincent Y. C. Shih, *op. cit.*, p. 32, n. 5.

3. See n. 18 to ch. II.

4. *Chung-kuo hsin-wen-hsüeh ti yüan-liu*, p. 10. This approximates the very simple and appropriate definition in William J. Long, *English Literature, Its History and Its Significance for the Life of the English-Speaking World* (Boston, 1909), p. 8: "Literature is the expression of life in words of truth and beauty, . . . its object, aside from the delight it gives us, is to know man, that is the soul of man rather than his action."

5. "Hsin wen-hsüeh ti yao-ch'iu," *Chung-kuo hsin-wen-hsüeh ta-hsi*, II, p. 155.

6. It is C. T. Hsia, *A History of Modern Chinese Fiction*, p. 19, who calls it "a crucial document"; it is similarly emphasized by Li Tien-yi, "Continuity and Change in Modern Chinese Literature," *Annals of the American Academy of Political and Social Science*, CCCXXI (1959), 92.

7. "Ko-hsing ti wen-hsüeh," *T'an-lung-chi*, p. 251.

8. "Shen-hua ti pien-hu," *Yü-t'ien ti shu*, p. 24.

9. "Wen-hsüeh yü chu-i, "*Yü-ssu*, no. 119 (February 19, 1927).

10. "Wen-hsüeh t'an," *T'an-lung-chi*, pp. 165-67. See also *Chou Tso-jen san-wen ch'ao*, p. 6, where Fei-ming states that Chou condemned the "proletarian literary movement as being too doctrinaire" ("tsai tao p'ai").

11. "Shih ti hsiao-yung," *Tzu-chi ti yüan-ti*, p. 21.

12. "T'o-lo hsü," *K'u-yü-chai hsü pa wen*, p. 36. Also see "Jih-pen shih-jen I-ch'a ti shih," *Hsiao-shuo yüeh-pao*, XII, no. 11 (November, 1921).

13. Preface to *I-shu yü sheng-huo*, p. 3-4. The same idea has been expressed by Wilamowitz: "true translation is a metempsychosis"; quoted from Theodore Savory, *The Art of Translation* (London, 1957), p. 48.

14. *Chung-kuo hsin-wen-hsüeh ta-hsi*, VII, pp. 191-94.

15. Chou quotes *Meng-tzu*, VII, pt. 2, p. 5: "A carpenter or a cartwright may give a man the circle and the square, but cannot make him skillful in the use of them." Legge, p. 356.

16. The phrase occurs in T'ao Yüan-ming's poem "On Moving House," which W. Acker, *T'ao the Hermit*, p. 60, translates: "Joyfully we will praise rare poetry together and settle doubtful meanings by mutual discussion."

17. Anatole France, *Oeuvres Complètes* (Paris, 1926,) vol. VI, "La vie littéraire," pp. 5-6. In his essay "Wen-i p'i-p'ing tsa-hua," Chou quotes this passage in Chinese translation at much greater length. The English rendering used in the text is the translation by James Lewis May in his *Anatole France, the Man and His Work* (London, 1924), p. 190.

Appendix

1. A literal translation of the title would be: "to collide with something and suffer injury."

2. Chou An-shih refers to Chou Meng-yen, whose courtesy name was An-shih; see Ts'ai Kuan-lo, *Ch'ing-tai ch'i-pai ming-jen chuan* (Hong Kong, 1963), p. 1529.

3. The book entitled *Yin-chih-wen*, author unknown, is mentioned in Morohashi, *op. cit.*, XI, 846, and also in Kyoto Daigaku Jimbun Kagaku Kenkyujō, *Hansei bunrui mokuroku* (1963 ed.) I, 681, among books on popular ethics.

4. The story of Sun Shu-ao and the double-headed snake may be found in Liu Hsiang (79–8, B.C.), *Hsin hsü*, third story of ch. I (Ts'ung-shu chi-ch'eng edition, p. 2). Sun Shu-ao is also mentioned in ch. CXIX of the *Shih-chi*.

5. On knight errantry in China, see James J. Y. Liu, *The Chinese Knight-Errant* (Chicago, 1967).

6. The Hsin Hua Gate is the Southern Gate leading into the Nan Hai and Chung Hai sections of Peking, which were districts of government and administrative buildings.

7. In view of the customary chaotic conditions on small Chinese

passenger crafts, Chou's statement must be taken as sardonic ridicule of the government statement.

8. The writers of funerary scrolls tried to demonstrate their erudition by quoting from classical literature, sometimes with doubtful results. The first part of the present inscription seems an adaptation from *Shih-chi, ch.* LXV, where a similarly worded phrase occurs, namely, "all in the boat were enemies." The expression *ch'ing liu* for "exalted élite" occurs in several places in classical literature; see Morohashi, *op. cit.,* VII, 75. Chou Tso-jen in quoting this scroll inscription must have also felt it to be an odd specimen of the scroll writers' art.

9. This refers to the incident on January 9, 1905, when about one thousand demonstrators were killed by troops guarding the czar's Winter Palace near Leningrad.

10. Refers to Ts'ui Hsü (1767–1846), whose courtesy name was Hsiao-lin and whose sobriquet was Nien-t'ang, which explains the title of his book, the *Nien-t'ang Shih-hua* (Random Notes on Poetry by Nien-t'ang). He is not listed in the standard biographical dictionaries.

11. The *Jih-chih-lu* is the best known work of the leading scholar of the early Ch'ing period, Ku Yen-wu (1613–82), whose sobriquet was T'ing-lin; see Hummel, *op. cit.,* p. 421: the *Jih-chih-lu* is a "collection of carefully written notes on a great variety of topics," first printed in 1670.

12. This book contains the works of Hsü Wei (1521–93), whose courtesy name was Wen-ch'ang, also Wen-ch'ing. He called himself Ch'ing-t'eng-shan-jen; see T'an Pi-wu, *op. cit.,* no. 4421.

13. T'an Yang is the sobriquet of Wang T'ao-chen, daughter of Wang Hsi-chüeh (see note 15), Morohashi, *op. cit.,* V, 937, where her sobriquet is given as T'an-yang-tzu; she became a disciple of a Buddhist after her fiancé died before the wedding.

14. The "Yellow Millet Dream" is an ancient story of magic and myth, symbolizing the transitoriness of world glory; see Morohashi, *ibid.,* XII, p. 980. It was also dramatized and is for instance mentioned in Fu Hsi-hua, *Yüan-tai tsa-chü ch'üan-mu* (Peking, 1957), pp. 72-73.

15. Wang Hsi-chüeh (1534–1610) was a man of T'ai-ts'ang; see T'an Pi-wu, *op. cit.,* no. 4573.

16. The *Yüeh-yen* is a book on customs and folklore of the Shao-hsing area, compiled by Fan Yin, whose courtesy name was Hsiao-feng, first published in 1882 and republished in 1932 with a postscript by Chou Tso-jen. It is listed in the Tōhō Bunka Kenkyujō catalog (1945), p. 296.

17. See note 11.

18. This refers to a story of Hsiao Wu Ti, emperor of the Liang

dynasty; see Morohashi, *op. cit.*, IX, p. 664: "In his sickness his mouth was bitter and he asked for honey. When he could not get it, he uttered a "ho ho" [of anger or anguish?] and died."

19. Hara Sen, whose courtesy name was Kōdō, compiled the *Sentetsu sōdan*, published in 1805; see *Nippon bungaku daijiten*, IV, 340. The *Sentetsu sōdan* is a biographical dictionary of scholars of the Edo period (1603–1867).

20. This refers to Chu Chih-yü, whose sobriquet was Shun-shui (1600–82); see Hummel, *op. cit.*, p. 179.

21. The *Hsien-hua Yang-chou* (Idle Talk of Yangchow) by I Chün-tso (Shanghai, 1935) is a casual account of gossip, customs, and life in Yangchow.

22. The term *ti-ting* that Chou uses here is not listed in general or botanical dictionaries and may be a Shaohsing colloquialism. That it refers to violets is evident from Lu Hsün's translation of Heinrich Heine's "Die blauen Veilchen der Äugelein. . . ." into "mou-tzu ch'ing ti ting. . . ." See A-ying, ed., *Wan Ch'ing Wen-hsüeh ts'ung-ch'ao*, Volume *Yü-wai wen-hsüeh i-wen*, I, 18. Chou Tso-jen mentions the *ti-ting* flower again in *Yeh-tu-ch'ao*, p. 152, line 11, and in *T'an-lung-chi*, p. 191, line 10.

23. Friedrich Fröbel (1782–1852) was the German educational reformer who is considered the founder of the kindergarten; see S. J. Curtis in *Encyclopaedia Britannica*, 1964 ed., IX, 951, and references there.

24. This refers to Mrs. Mary Godwin, née Wollstonecraft (1759–97), thought of as a radical in her time because of her fight for the *Vindication of the Rights of Women* (title of her book; 1792) and also of her advanced *Thoughts on the Education of Daughters* (another book by her; 1787); see W. M. Merchant in *Encyclopaedia Britannica* 1964 ed., X, 518-519, and references there.

25. William Blake (1787–1827), a colorful personality, both poet and graphic artist, with strong mystic and metaphysical tendencies; see G. L. Keynes in *Encyclopaedia Britannica*, 1964 ed., III, 756-59. Blake's *The Marriage of Heaven and Hell* was published in 1793.

26. The Chinese dictionary *Tz'u-yüan*, vol. 1, section "mao," p. 27, gives a quotation from Han Yü as the origin of the phrase "pei t'ien min jen" (have pity on the world and commiserate the people), now used simply for "avoir compassion pour qn., avoir pitié de qn., s'apitoyer." See *Dictionnaire Chinois-Français* (Peking, 1960), p. 15.

27. *Lun-yü*, VI, para. 28, which, in Legge's translation, reads: "Suppose the case of a man extensively conferring benefits on the people, and able to assist all. . . ."

28. Mo-tzu or Mo-ti (fl. 400 B.C.), philosopher of the Confucian school who propounded the concept of "universal love" as the ethical

basis of his philosophy; see Legge, *Chinese Classics,* II, prolegomena pp. 103 ff.

29. The *jou-p'u-t'uan* (Prayer Mat of Flesh) is a pornographic novel attributed to Li Yü (1611–80?); see Hummel, *op. cit.,* p. 496. It has been translated into French, German, and English; see a discussion of the book by Jeremy Ingalls, "Mr. Ch'ing-yin and the Chinese Erotic Novel," *Yearbook of Comparative and General Literature,* XIII (1964), pp. 60-63.

30. *Chiu-wei-kuei* is a modern erotic novel; see *Hu Shih wen-ts'un,* I, 197.

31. The books quoted are commonly known among educated Chinese; they can all be identified in A. Wylie, *Notes on Chinese Literature,* and in Morohashi, *op. cit.*

32. Cf. J. J. M. de Groot, *The Religious System of China,* vol. II, pp. 735–69, "Sutteeism; Widowhood."

33. Tsuda Sōkichi (1873–1961) had his *Bungaku ni arawaretaru kokumin shisō no kenkyū* (Study of National Thought as Revealed in Literature) published in Tokyo in four volumes, 1918–21; see *Bunka jimmei roku,* 1963, p. 722.

34. Kuo Chü of the later Han period is mentioned as one of the twenty-four examples of filial piety, because he killed his son in order to be better able to provide for his mother during a famine; see Morohashi, *op. cit.,* XI, 261.

35. Ting Lan of the later Han period is said to have carved a wooden image of his deceased mother in order to be able to continue his services to her; see Morohashi, *op. cit.,* I, 78, and sources given there.

36. This is another story of extreme filial piety; see Morohashi, *op. cit.,* II, 301, and sources cited there. Cf. also J. J. M. de Groot, *op. cit.,* v. 4, pp. 386-87, "People curing their parents with their flesh."

37. Hu Chin-t'ang refers to Hu Yin (1098–1156); see T'an Cheng-pi *Chung-kuo wen-hsüeh-chia ta tz'u-tien,* p. 681 (no. 2386). He was a high official involved in policy struggles during the defense of the Sung dynasty against the incursions of the northern barbarians.

38. Emperor Ch'ien Lung reigned 1736–96; Hummel, *op. cit.,* pp. 369-73. Many of his edicts restricted publication of writings deemed critical of the Manchu regime; cf. L. C. Goodrich, *The Literary Inquisition of Ch'ien-lung* (Baltimore: Waverly Press, 1935).

Selected Bibliography

PRIMARY SOURCES

No complete collection of all of Chou Tso-jen's works has so far been published. Out of over seventy books known to contain his writings the following thirty-one seem to be the most notable ones:

Yü-wai hsiao-shuo chi (Collection of Foreign Short Stories) Translations, first published in Tokyo, 1909, republished in Shanghai, 1920, with a preface by Chou Tso-jen; again published in Peking, 1935. Part of the translations by Lu Hsün.

Tien-ti (Drops) Collection of translated short stories. National Peking University Press, 1920.

Tzu-chi ti yüan-ti (One's Own Garden). Peking, 1923 and 1934.

Ming-shih lü-hsing (Travels in the Underworld). Peking, 1925.

Yü-t'ien ti shu (A Rainy Day's Book). Peking, 1925.

I-shu yü sheng-huo (Art and Life). Peking, 1926.

K'uang-yen shih fan (Ten *kyogen* Plays). Peking, 1926.

T'an-lung-chi (Speaking of Dragons). Peking, 1927.

Tse-hsieh-chi (The Water-plantain). Shanghai, 1927.

T'an-hu-chi (Speaking of Tigers). Peking, 1928.

Chou Tso-jen san-wen ch'ao (Collection of Chou Tso-jen's Essays), selected by Chang Hsi-shen. Shanghai, 1932.

Chung-kuo hsin wen-hsüeh ti yüan-liu (The Sources of China's Modern Literature). Peking, 1932. Republished Hong Kong, 1955, under the title *Chung-kuo chin-tai wen-hsüeh shih hua* (On Modern Chinese Literature).

K'an-yün-chi ("Gazing at the Clouds" Collection). Shanghai, 1932.

Chih-t'ang wen-chi (A Collection of Chih-t'ang's Writings). Shanghai, 1933.

Chou Tso-jen shu-hsin (Letters of Chou Tso-jen). Shanghai, 1933; reprinted Hong Kong, 1967.

Yeh-tu-ch'ao (Notes from Night Reading). Shanghai, 1934.

Chou Tso-jen wen-hsüan-chi (Selected Writings of Chou Tso-jen), ed. by Shao Hou. Shanghai, 1936.

Chou Tso-jen hsüan-chi (Selected Writings by Chou Tso-jen), ed. by Hsü Shen-ssu and Yeh Wang-yu. Shanghai, 1936.
Kua-tou-chi ("Melons and Beans" Collection). Shanghai, 1937.
Ping-chu-t'an (Talks by Candlelight). Shanghai, 1940.
Yao-t'ang yü-lu (Jottings by Yao-t'ang). Tientsin, 1941.
Yao-wei-chi ("Bitter Taste" Collection). Peking, 1942.
K'u-k'ou kan-k'ou (Bitter and Sweet). Shanghai, 1944.
Shu-fang i-chiao (A Corner of the Library). Peking, 1944.
Yao-t'ang tsa-wen (Random Essays of Yao-t'ang). Peking, 1944.
Ping-chu hou-t'an (Talks by Candlelight, Continuation). Shanghai, 1944.
Li-ch'un i-ch'ien (Before Spring). Shanghai, 1945.
Lu Hsün ti ku chia (Lu Hsün's Old Home). Shanghai, 1953.
Lu Hsün hsiao-shuo li ti jen-wu (The Characters in Lu Hsün's Novels). Shanghai, 1954; republished in Hong Kong, undated.
Lu Hsün ti ch'ing-nien shih-tai (Lu Hsün's Youth). Peking, 1957.
Chih-t'ang i-yu wen-pien (Chih-t'ang's Writings During 1945). Hong Kong, 1961.

SECONDARY SOURCES

ANDO KŌSEI. "Ku'usai hōmonki" (A Visit to Chou Tso-jen's Studio), *Daian Monthly,* no. 98 (January, 1964), 1-4.
CHENG TZU-YÜ. "Chou shih hsiung-ti hsin-shih yen-chiu" (Study of the Modern-Style Poetry of the Chou Brothers), *Tung-tu hsi-chiang lu.* Singapore, 1963, pp. 43-60.
CHIN TIEN-JUNG. "Chou Tso-jen Kuan I-hsien hsing t'ao ssu hsing chi" (Chou Tso-jen and Kuan I-hsien's Lucky Escape from the Death Penalty), *Ch'un-ch'iu tsa-chih,* no. 197 (Hong Kong; September 15, 1965), 5-7.
CHU P'U (under his pen name Hsing-chai) "I chih-t'ang lao jen" (Memories of Chou Tso-jen), *Ta-hua* (magazine), no. 28 (Hong Kong; April 30, 1967), 1-3.
FANG CHI-SHENG, comp. *Shu Saku-jin sensei no koto* (On Chou Tso-jen). A collection of biographic essays by various friends and colleagues. Tokyo, 1944.
HIGUCHI SUSUMU. "Shu Saku-jin shiron" (Essay on Chou Tso-jen), *Chugoku gakuron shū.* Tokyo, 1964.
HUANG PO-SSU. "Cho Tso-jen ti chi pen shu" (On Some Books by Chou Tso-jen), *Ta-kung-pao* (newspaper), Shanghai edition, October 25, 1946.
HUANG SHANG. "Keng t'an Chou Tso-jen" (More on Chou Tso-jen) and "Lao-hu-ch'iao pien k'an Chih-t'ang" (Meeting Chou Tso-jen at the Nanking Prison), both in his *Chin-fan chi-wai.* Shanghai, 1948.

IIKURA SHŌHEI. "Shuki no Shu Saku-jin ni tsuite no nōto" (Notes on Chou Tso-jen's Early Period), *Kobe Daigaku bungakukai kenkyū,* no. 38 (November, 1966) and no. 40 (November 1967).

LIANG SHIH-CH'IU. "Wu-ssu yü wen-i" (The May Fourth Movement and Literature), Wen-hsüeh yin-yüan. Taipei, 1964.

LIN YUTANG. "Chi Chou shih hsiung-ti" (Memories of the Chou Brothers), *Chung-yang jih-pao* (newspaper), Taipei, March 26, 1965.

LIU HSIN-HUANG. "Kuan-yü Chou Tso-jen" (About Chou Tso-jen) *Ch'uang-tso,* no. 1 (Taipei; August, 1961), 81-85.

MASUDA WATARU. "Shu Saku-jin ron" (On Chou Tso-jen), *Chūgoku bungaku geppō,* IX (November 27, 1935), 97-98.

POLLARD, D. E. "Chou Tso-jen and Cultivating One's Garden," *Asia Major,* N.S. XI (1965), 180-98.

SHANGRAW, SYLVIA. "A Study of the Early Essays of Chou Tso-jen, 1918-1934," unpubl. M.A. Thesis at the University of California (Berkeley, 1965).

SU HSÜEH-LIN. "Shen-shih liu-mang ch'i-chih ko pan ti Chou Tso-jen" (The Gentleman-Vagabond Chou Tso-jen), *Wen-t'an hua-chiu.* Taipei, 1967.

TA FANG. "Chou Tso-jen chiao-shu mai-wen i erh shih" (Some Random Notes on Chou Tso-jen's Teaching and Writing), *Ch'un-ch'iu tsa-chih,* no. 198 (October 1, 1965), 10.

T'AO MING-CHIA, ed. *Chou Tso-jen* (On Chou Tso-jen). A collection of essays on various aspects of Chou's work by friends and critics. Shanghai, 1934.

Index

Sex and sex mores, 40, 52, 53

Shanghai, 6, 11, 23, 72, 77

Shao-nien Chung-kuo (Young China), 3

Shaohsing, 1, 3, 20, 33, 35, 70, 72, 75, 92

Shen-pao (newspaper), 79

Shih-shuo hsin-yü (Sayings of the World), 13

Shih Wei, 32

Shinto, 66

Shirakaba (White Birch) literary school, 4, 64, 67

Shui-hu (Water Margin), 16

"Sinism," 56, 57

Six Dynasties period, 13, 14

Socrates, 54, 55

Sologub, Fedor, 63

Spencer, Herbert, 20, 41

Ssu-k'ung T'u, 25

Stevenson, R. L. B., 38

Stopes, Marie, 40

Strindberg, Johann August, 63

Students' Anti-Religious Movement, 61

Su Man-shu, 18

Su-pao (newspaper), 60

Su Shih (Su Tung-p'o), 10, 14

Su Ti-jen, 9

Suderman, Hermann, 104

Sun Fu-yüan, 4

Sun Shu-ao, 90

suttee, 102, 103

Swift, Jonathan, 31, 38, 63

Tagore, Rabindranath, 102

Taiwan, vii, 11

Taku'an, 76

T'ang dynasty, 37, 74; collectanea, 90; poetry, 86

T'ang Erh-ho, 9

T'ao Ch'ien (T'ao Yüan-ming), 14, 27, 79, 87

Taoism and Taoists, 51, 57, 58, 101

Taylor, E. B., 41

Tea and tea ceremony, 27, 73-76

Tientsin, 77

Tokyo, 35, 36, 41, 43, 44

Tolstoy, L. N., 102

Translating, 58, 68

Translations, from European writers, 42, 44, 47, 63-64; from Japanese, 67-69

tsai-tao literary philosophy, 83

Ts'ai Yüan-p'ei, 3

Ts'ao Pi, 13

Tsuda Sōkichi, 104

Ts'ui Hsiao-lin, 92

Tuan Ch'i-jui, 5, 46, 60, 77

Turgenev, I. S., 125

Ueda, Kyōsuke, 74

Voltaire, 27, 54, 95

Wang An-shih, 14

Wang Ch'ung, 19, 25

Wang Hsi-chih, 14

Wang Wei, 27

Wang Yang-ming, 19

Wen-hsüan, 14

Wen-hsüeh chou-pao (Literary Weekly), 63

Wen-yen (the literary language), 22, 24

Westermarck, Edward Alexander, 41, 102

Western civilization, 20, 34

Western literature, 17, 83

Western thought, 17, 37, 38

Wilde, Oscar, 96

Wolff, Christian, 54

Yang Hsi-fu, 55

Yang Jen-shan, 57

Yangtse river, 91

Yasuoka Hideo, 66

Yen-chih literary philosophy, 83, 84

Yen Fu, 17, 37

Yosano Akiko, 67

Yü Cheng-hsieh, 19, 20

Yü-chou-feng (The Cosmic Wind), 6-8

Yü-ssu (Threads of Talk), 4, 48, 62, 63

Yü Ta-fu, 28, 53, 79

Yü-yao (district of Chekiang Province), 94

Zeromski, Stephan, 63